Practical Web Test Automation

Test web applications wisely with open source test frameworks: Watir and Selenium WebDriver

Zhimin Zhan

Practical Web Test Automation

Test web applications wisely with open source test frameworks: Watir and Selenium WebDriver

Zhimin Zhan

This book is for sale at
http://www.amazon.com/Practical-Web-Test-Automation-applications/dp/1505882893

This version was published on 2015-11-05

ISBN 978-1-50-588289-6

Leanpub

This is a Leanpub book. Leanpub empowers authors and publishers with the Lean Publishing process. Lean Publishing is the act of publishing an in-progress ebook using lightweight tools and many iterations to get reader feedback, pivot until you have the right book and build traction once you do.

©2012 - 2015 Zhimin Zhan

Also By Zhimin Zhan

Watir Recipes

Selenium WebDriver Recipes in Ruby

Selenium WebDriver Recipes in Java

Learn Ruby Programming by Examples

Selenium WebDriver Recipes in C#

Selenium WebDriver Recipes in Python

I dedicate this book to my mother and father for their unconditional love.

Contents

Preface i
    Who should read this book? ii
    How to read this book? iii
    What's inside the book? iii
    Test scripts, Screencasts and Other resources iv
    Send Me Feedback iv
    Acknowledgements iv

1. **What is Web Test Automation?** 1
    Test Automation Benefits 1
    Reality Check 2
    Reasons for Test Automation Failures 3
    Successful Web Test Automation 5
    Learning Approach 5
    Next Action 6

2. **First Automated Test** 7
    Test Design 7
    Installing TestWise (about 2 minutes) 8
    Create a Test 10
    Create Test Case From Recorded Test Steps 13
    Run test in IE 14
    When a test failed… 15
    Wrap up 17

3. **How Automated Testing works** 19
    Web Test Drivers 20
    Automated Testing Rhythm 22
    Test Frameworks 28

CONTENTS

    Run Tests From Command Line 32

4. **TestWise - Functional Testing IDE** **35**
    Philosophy of TestWise 35
    TestWise Project Structure 36
    Test Execution 37
    Keyboard Navigation 38
    Snippets 39
    Script Library 40
    Test Refactoring 40
    Wrap Up 41

5. **Case Study** **43**
    Test Site 43
    Preparation 43
    Create Test Project 44
    Test Suite: Sign in 45
    Test Suite: Select Flights 49
    Enter Passenger Details 54
    Book confirmation after payment 58
    Run all tests 60
    Wrap Up 62

6. **Test Automation Characteristics** **63**
    Specific 63
    Clean 64
    Independent 67
    Frequent 68
    Focused 69
    Programmable 72
    Creative 75
    Sustainable 76
    Wrap Up 77

7. **Maintainable Functional Test Design** **79**
    Record/Playback Leads to Unmaintainable Test Scripts . . . 79
    Success Criteria 80
    Maintainable Automated Test Design 81
    Maintain with Ease 84

	Case Study: Refine Test Scripts	84
	Wrap Up	91
8.	**Functional Test Refactoring**	**93**
	Code Refactoring	93
	Functional Test Refactoring	93
	Tool Support	94
	Case Study	94
	Summary	105
9.	**Review**	**107**
	Syntax Errors	107
	Set up source control	109
	GUI/Object Map	112
	Custom Libraries	112
	Debugging	113
10.	**Collaboration**	**115**
	Pre-requisite	115
	Scenario 1: "It worked on my machine"	116
	Scenario 2: Synergy	118
	Scenario 3: Acceptance Test Driven Development	122
	Wrap up	127
11.	**Continuous Integration with Functional Tests**	**129**
	Long feedback loop	129
	Continuous Integration	131
	Continuous Integration and Testing	131
	CI Build Steps	131
	Functional UI Test Build Step with Rake	133
	Set up a continuous testing server: BuildWise	135
	Review	143
	Dynamic Build Process	144
12.	**Test Reporting**	**147**
	Reporting Automated Test Results	147
	Defect Tracking	149
	Requirement Traceability	150

CONTENTS

13. Selenium **157**
    Selenium Framework 157
    Case Study: Switch RWebSpec to use Selenium 160
    Run in Firefox on Mac 165
    Case Study: Selenium-WebDriver and RSpec 166
    Cross Browser Functional Testing 174
    Comparison: Selenium and Watir 175

14. Cucumber **179**
    Cucumber Framework 179
    Case Study: Selenium and Cucumber 180
    Comparison: RSpec and Cucumber 190
    RSpec and Cucumber Co-exists 190

15. Adopting Test Automation **193**
    Seek Executive Sponsorship 193
    Choose Test Framework 194
    Select Test Tool 196
    Find a Mentor 197
    Manage Expectation 198
    Solo Test Automation 198
    Common Mistakes 199
    Wrap up 205

Appendix 1 Functional Test Refactoring Catalog **207**
    Move Test Scripts 207
    Extract Function 212
    Extract to Page Class 217
    Introduce Page Object 220
    Rename 222

Appendix 2 Test Automation in ClinicWise project **225**
    Build Stats 225
    Stage 1: Write automated tests on the first day 228
    Stage 2: Set up CI server within the first week 228
    Stage 3: Release to production early 228
    Stage 4: Release often (daily) 229
    Stage 5: Set up parallel test execution in CI 230
    Questions and Answers 231

Resources **235**
    Books 235
    Web Sites 235
    Tools 236

References **237**

Preface

On April 3 2013, Wired published an article "The Software Revolution Behind LinkedIn's Gushing Profits"[1]. The revolution "completely overhauled how LinkedIn develops and ships new updates to its website and apps, taking a system that required a full month to release new features and turning it into one that pushes out updates multiple times per day." LinkedIn is not alone, Google has accomplished this long before that. As a matter of fact, LinkedIn's success is tracked back to luring a Google veteran in 2001. "Facebook is released twice a day"[2] and they claimed "keeping up this pace is at the heart of our culture"[3].

Release software twice a day! For many, that's unimaginable. You may wonder how they could ensure quality (and you know the high standard from them). The answer is, as the article pointed out, using "automated tests designed to weed out any bugs."

After working on numerous software projects for a number of years, I witnessed and had been part of many what I call 'release panic syndromes'. That is, with the deadline approaching, the team's panic level rises. Many defects were found from the last round of manual testing by the testers, the manager started prioritizing the defects (or adjusting some to features), and programmers rushing to fix just the critical ones. Testers restarted the testing on the new build which fixed some but not all the defects. Then here came the bad news: several previously working features were now broken, Argh!

I believe there is a better way to do software development that does not involve this kind of stress and panic. This is how my interest in automated testing started (in 2006). I made the right decision to use free, open source and programming based test frameworks. (It is quite obvious now, as Selenium is the best sought after testing skill on the job market. Back then, people turned to record/playback commercial tools with vendor proprietary test script syntax). The first test framework I used (for my pet projects) was Watir. Wow! I was convinced that this approach was the answer.

In 2007, I had the opportunity to put my approach into practices in a government project. The outcome was beyond everyone's expectation: over two years and countless releases, there were no major defects reported by customers. The team had high confidence in the product. These automated tests also provided the safety net for some major refactorings, which would

---
[1] http://www.wired.com/business/2013/04/linkedin-software-revolution/
[2] http://www.facebook.com/notes/facebook-engineering/ship-early-and-ship-twice-as-often/10150985860363920
[3] http://www.seleniumconf.org/speakers/

not be possible without them. A business analyst once said, "before every demonstration to our customers, it is a good feeling of knowing every release has been thoroughly tested." The synergy of flexible test framework, maintainable test design, team collaboration with the same simple testing tool and continuous integration supporting functional test execution really made a big difference.

There is now a clearly converging trend in web application development on technology choices, such as cloud deployment, light and productive web frameworks such as "Ruby on Rails"[4], JQuery JavaScript Library, Twitter BootStrap UI themes, Font Awesome icons, ..., etc. The competitions among web applications are less on technologies, but weigh more on the development process to ensure pushing out high quality releases often. A fact: Facebook was not the first social networking web site.

A friend of mine, who developed a quite successful public web application, told me in an uneasy tone that he just found out another competitor product at a cheaper price. This is inevitable, the competition among web applications is global, which means, there are people work at 10% of your hourly rate to compete against you. The only way to win the race, in my opinion, is to greatly enhance your productivity and reduce maintenance cost. This can be achieved by applying test automation and continuous integration with instant benefits without much effort (if doing it properly). My reply to my friend: "If your competitors seriously start to invest in test automation, you shall be worried."

In Appendix II, I share my experience on developing ClinicWise, a modern web-based clinic management system. Thanks to comprehensive automated UI testing, ClinicWise is frequently released (daily) with new features and updates. ClinicWise is developed and maintained in my spare time.

The motivation of this book is to share my journey of test automation for web applications: from writing the first test to developing and maintaining large number of automated test scripts.

Who should read this book?

Everyone working on a software team (including testers, programmers, business analysts, architects and managers) building a web application who wants to improve the quality of software while saving time and money can benefit from reading this book. It may sound like a bold statement, but it is the outcome I obtained from some projects whose team members

---

[4]http://yourstory.com/2013/02/startup-technologies-top-6-technologies-used-at-startups/

embraced the techniques and practices presented in this book. Those projects delivered reliable software releases frequently, stress free. You can achieve this too.

Prior experience with automated testing is not necessary. Basic programming concepts will help, but again, not necessary.

How to read this book?

I strongly recommend readers to read through Chapters 1-9 in order, only skip Chapter 4 if you have decided on the testing editor/IDE. Chapters 10-15 are largely independent from one another. You can therefore read them in the order that suits your interests. Readers can also just skim through and come back for details later if necessary.

Some chapters contain hands-on exercises (with step by step guides). Typically it will take about 10-30 minutes to complete an exercise. Readers can choose to follow the exercises while or after reading a chapter. The main point is: to master test automation, you have to do it.

What's inside the book?

In part 1, I introduce Web Test Automation and its benefits, which many believe but few actually achieve it. I use a metaphor to illustrate practical reasons why most software projects conduct functional testing manually despite knowing the great benefits of test automation. Then the journey starts with a case study to help write your first Watir automated test in about 10 minutes.

In part 2, I present a brief introduction of test frameworks and tools, followed by a case study showing the development of six Watir/RWebSpec[5] tests for a live test site with the help of a recorder. Along the way, some testing techniques are introduced.

In part 3, I present an intuitive and maintainable automated test design: using reusable functions and page objects, followed by a case study showing the transforming of recorded test scripts to a maintainable way. Then I introduce an important concept: functional test refactoring, a process of testers applying refactorings to test scripts efficiently with refactoring support in testing tools such as TestWise IDE[6].

With a growing number of automated tests, so is the test execution time. Long feedback loops really slow down development. In part 4, I show how team collaboration and continuous integration can help to improve the feedback time greatly.

---

[5]https://github.com/zhimin/rwebspec
[6]http://testwisely.com

In Part 5, I switch the attention to two other frameworks: Selenium-WebDriver[7] and Cucumber[8], with two case studies showing the test design and techniques are applicable generally. Finally I share some strategies to apply test automation to your project.

Test scripts, Screencasts and Other resources

To help readers learn more effectively, the book has a dedicated site at: http://zhimin.com/books/pwta[9], which contains the following resources:

- **Software**. Test automation is not necessarily expensive. All test frameworks featured in this book are free and open-sourced. Testing tools used for the exercises in this book are also free, and there are instructions to cater for other text-based testing tools.
- **Sample test scripts**. The sample test scripts for the exercises are ready-to-run. This book covers several popular test and syntax frameworks: Watir, Selenium, RWebSpec, RSpec and Cucumber. To help readers understand the differences, I have created 8 test projects with different combinations: https://github.com/zhimin/adminwise-ui-tests[10].
- **Sample web sites**. For readers who need web sites to try out automated test scripts, I have prepared two test sites for you:
    - *Agile Travel*: a simple flight booking site, which is used in the exercises.
    - *AdminWise*: a feature rich web 2.0 site with modules such as membership and library.
- **Tutorial screencasts**. There are screencasts for readers who learn better with audio and video, so you will be able to see how it is done step by step.

Send Me Feedback

I'd appreciate hearing from you. Comments, suggestions, errors in the book and test scripts are all welcome. You can submit your feedback on the book web site (http://zhimin.com/books/pwta).

Acknowledgements

I would like to thank everyone who sent feedback and suggestions, particularly Darren James, Mingli Zhou, Tim Wilson, Lloyd Blake, Hoang Uong and Lien Nguyen, for their time and wisdom.

---

[7] http://seleniumhq.org/
[8] http://cukes.info/
[9] http://zhimin.com/books/pwta
[10] https://github.com/zhimin/adminwise-ui-tests

I owe a huge 'thank you' to people behind great open-source testing frameworks such as Watir, Selenium-WebDriver and RSpec, and of course, the beautiful Ruby language.

Functional testing via User Interface is practical and light on theory, so is this book. I hope you find this book useful.

Zhimin Zhan
May 2014

1. What is Web Test Automation?

Web Test Automation, or automated functional testing for web applications via the Graphical User Interface (GUI), is the use of automated test scripts to drive test executions to verify that the web application meets its requirements. Simply, during execution of an automated test for a web site, you see mouse and keyboard actions such as clicking a button and typing text in a text box in a browser, without human intervention. Web Test Automation sits under the category of black-box functional testing, where the majority of test efforts is in software projects.

> **Functional Testing vs Unit Testing vs Non-Functional Testing**
>
> Functional testing is to verify function requirements: *what* the system does. For example, "User can request a password reset by providing a valid email". This is the focus of this book.
>
> Unit testing is a type of white box testing performed by programmers at source code level. It is of no concerns to software testers. Unit test is a term that gets misused a lot. A more correct term would be "Programmer Test". A product that passes comprehensive programmer tests can still fail on many functional tests. That's because programmers tests are from a programmer's perspective, while functional tests are from a user's perspective. A programmer test is also a kind of automated test.
>
> Non-functional testing is the testing of *how* the system works. For example, "The response time of the home page must not exceed 5 seconds." Some type of non-functional testings, load testing in particular, utilize automated test tools too.

Test Automation Benefits

The benefits of test automation are many. Below are four common ones:

- **Reliable**. Tests perform precisely the same operations each time they are run, thereby eliminating human errors.

- **Fast**. Test execution is faster than done manually.
- **Repeatable**. Once tests are created, they can be run repeatedly with little effort, even at lunch time or after working hours.
- **Regression Testing**. "The intent of regression testing is to ensure that a change, such as a bug fix, did not introduce new faults" [Myers, Glenford 04]. Comprehensive manual regression testing is almost impossible to conduct for two reasons: the time required and human errors. As Steve McConnell pointed out, "The only practical way to manage regression testing is to automate it." [McConnell]

What do I like about test automation?

If you want me to use only one adjective to describe web test automation, it is *fun*. I enjoy creating something that can I can get to do work for me. I have a habit of triggering execution of a test suite before going out for lunch. I like the feeling of "still working" while enjoying a meal. When I come back, a test report is already there, waiting for me.

Reality Check

With more software projects adopting agile methodologies and more software application developments moving towards the Web, you would assume web test automation would be everywhere now. The answer is, sadly, no. In fact, functional testing in many projects is still executed in pretty much the same way: manually.

UI Test Automation Tools are Snake Oil - Michael Feathers

It happens over and over again. I visit a team and I ask about their testing situation. We talk about unit tests, exploratory testing, the works. Then, I ask about automated end-to-end testing and they point at a machine in the corner. That poor machine has an installation of some highly-priced per seat testing tool (or an open source one, it doesn't matter), and the chair in front of it is empty. We walk over, sweep the dust away from the keyboard, and load up the tool. Then, we glance through their set of test scripts and try to run them. The system falls over a couple of times and then they give me that sheepish grin and say "we tried." I say, "don't worry, everyone does." [Feathers 10]

Reasons for Test Automation Failures

The software testing survey conducted by Innovative Defense Technologies in 2007 [IDT07] shows *"73% of survey respondents believe Automated Testing is beneficial but few automate"*. The top reasons for survey participants not automating their software testing efforts (while agreeing with the benefits) are:

- lack of time
- lack of budget
- lack of expertise

These reasons sound about right to most people. However, saving time and money are two benefits of test automation, isn't that a contradiction (for lack of time and budget)? What are the real difficulties or challenges, apart from political or project management ones, that projects encounter during their adventures in automated testing?

To make it easy to understand, we can compare a project's test automation attempt with a boy who is trying to climb over a standing two-hump camel from the front. Let's consider each of the following challenges he faces:

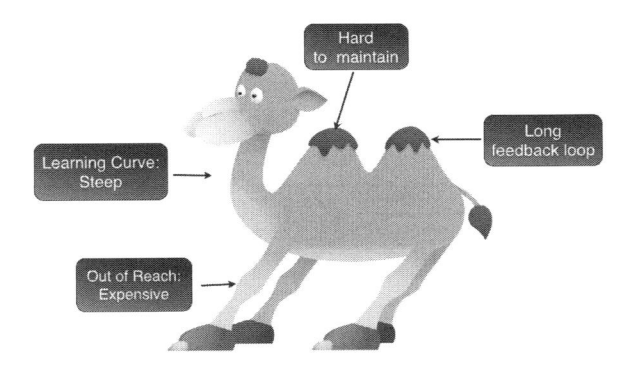

Test Automation Camel

Figure 1-1 Test Automation Camel (graphics credit: www.freevectordownload.com)

1. Out of reach: Expensive

Commercial testing tools are usually quite expensive (I won't list prices here, in fact, I couldn't get prices for some so-called leading testing tools on their web sites, which is telling in itself). Automated testing is one of a few activities in software projects that the whole team can contribute to and benefit from. Besides testers, programmers may run automated tests for self verification and business analysts may utilize automated tests for customer demonstrations. However, high price of commercial testing tools makes the whole team's adoption of automated testing unfeasible.

There are free, open-source testing frameworks, such as Selenium and Watir, both of which are featured in the classic book 'Agile Testing[1]' by Lis Crispin and Janet Gregory. However the idea of free and open-source testing frameworks is still not appealing to many test managers. Lack of skills, dedicated tools and support are their main concerns.

2. Steep Learning Curves: Difficult to learn

Traditional commercial tools are usually focused on a Record and Playback approach with test scripts in a vendor proprietary syntax. It looks easy when you watch the sales presentations. In real life, unfortunately, it is a quite different story (a programmer's minor change to the application can ruin your hours of recording). When testers have to open the raw test scripts (generated by recorders) to edit, reality bites.

Open source test frameworks, on the other hand, require some degree of programming efforts, Watir, Selenium and WebTest are among the popular ones. With programming, they provide flexibility needed for automated testing. However, the fact is that the majority of software testers do not possess programming skills, and many of them feel uncomfortable to learn it. There are few dedicated testing tools supporting these open-source test frameworks designed to suite testers. (Programming IDEs are designed for programmers, not for testers who can find them complicated and overwhelming).

3. Hump 1: Hard to maintain

Software under development changes frequently, and automated UI test scripts are vulnerable to application changes. Even a simplest change to the application could cause many existing test scripts fail. This, in my view, is the most fundamental reason for test automation failures.

4. Hump 2: Long feedback loop

Compared to programmer tests (which if written well, should have an execution time under 0.1 second), automated functional tests through UI are relatively slow. There is practically very little that testers can do to speed up execution of functional tests. With the number of test cases growing, so will be the test execution time. This leads to long feedback gap, from the time programmers committed the code to the time test execution completes. If programmers

---

[1] http://www.agiletester.ca/

continue developing new feature or fixes during the gap time, it can easily get into a tail-chasing problem. This will hurt team's productivity badly, not to mention team's morale.

New Challenges for testing Web applications

Specifically to web applications, with adoption of AJAX (Asynchronous JavaScript and XML) and increasing use of JavaScripts, websites nowadays are more dynamic, therefore, bringing new challenges to web test automation.

Successful Web Test Automation

Having identified the reasons for test automation failures in projects, it becomes clear what it takes to succeed in web test automation:

1. Test scripts must be easy to read and maintain.
2. Testing framework/tools are easy to learn, affordable and support team collaboration.
3. Test execution must be fast.

Is that all possible? My answer is 'Yes'. The purpose of this book is to show how we can achieve just that.

Learning Approach

This is not yet another book on testing theories, as there are no shortage of them. In this book, we will walk through examples using test framework RWebSpec, Watir or Selenium and functional testing IDE TestWise. The best way to learn is to just start doing it.

My father is a well respected high school mathematics teacher in our town, his teaching style is "teaching by examples". That is, he gets students to work on his carefully selected math exercises followed by concise instruction, then guide students who face challenges (often he gives them another exercise). That is also the way I learn things. By working with testers, I found this is the most effective way for testers to master automated testing quickly.

For most web sites, regardless of technologies they are developed on, Internet Explorer on Windows is often the target platform (at least for now). It will be the main platform for our exercises in this book:

Operating System:	Windows XP or later
Web Browser:	Internet Explorer v8-10 (*IE11 is not well supported yet*[2])
Test Framework:	Watir (with RWebSpec extension)
Testing Tool:	TestWise IDE

If you are Mac user, like myself, the learning process is the same (majority of the test scripts run without change) except the screenshots shown in the book look different.

Operating System:	Mac OS X
Web Browser:	Firefox or Chrome
Test Framework:	Selenium-WebDriver (with RWebSpec extension)
Testing Tool:	TestWise IDE Mac Edition

I will cover more on Selenium to drive tests against Firefox or Google Chrome Browser on Mac or Linux in Chapter 13 (I am a Mac user myself). All the techniques and even test scripts are directly applicable for cross-browser testing.

On testing tools, I use TestWise community edition, a free testing IDE supporting Watir and Selenium, in this book. For readers who prefer their favourite editors/IDEs, you can still use them, as all test scripts shown in this book are plain text. I will also provide instructions on how to execute tests from the command line.

Example test scripts for chapters in this book can be downloaded at http://zhimin.com/books/pwta[3], and you can try them out by simply opening in TestWise and run. Also, I have provided screencasts there so that readers can watch how it is done.

In this book, we will focus on testing standard web sites (in HTML), excluding vendor specific technologies such as Flash and SilverLight. The techniques shown in this book are applicable to general testing practices.

Next Action

Enough theory for now. Let's roll up sleeves and write some automated tests.

---

[2]https://code.google.com/p/selenium/wiki/InternetExplorerDriver#IE_11_Support
[3]http://zhimin.com/books/pwta

2. First Automated Test

"A journey of a thousand miles must begin with a single step." - Lao Tzu

Let's write an automated web test. If you are new to automated testing, don't feel intimidated. You are going to see your first automated test running in Internet Explorer in about 10 minutes, and that includes installing the test tool!

Test Design

A test starts with a requirement (called User Story in agile projects). Quite commonly, the first simple requirement to test is: User Authentication. We will use this requirement for our first test in this exercise.

By analysing the requirement and the application (see the screenshot below),

Agile travel login

we can start to collect the test data:

```
Site URL: http://travel.agileway.net
User Login/Password: agileway/testwise
```

and design the test steps:

1. Enter username "agileway"
2. Enter password "testwise"
3. Click button "Sign In"
4. Verify: "Login successful!" appears

You might by now be saying *"there is no difference from manual testing"*. That's correct. If you currently work as a manual tester, you probably feel a relief at knowing your test design skills apply to automated testing as well. As a matter of fact, we usually perform the test steps manually as verification of test design before writing automated test scripts.

Now we are going to automate it. The main purpose of this exercise is to help you write an automated Watir test case and watch it running in IE, in a matter of minutes. Don't pay attention to details yet, as it will become clear as we move on. If you get stuck, follow the screencast for this exercise at http://zhimin.com/books/pwta[1].

Installing TestWise (about 2 minutes)

We will use TestWise, a Functional Testing IDE, for this exercise. *(TestWise Community Edition is free)*

Prerequisite

- A PC with MS Windows XP/7/8
- TestWise recorder which requires Mozilla Firefox

Download

- *TestWise IDE Community Edition* from http://testwisely.com/testwise/downloads[2] (18MB download).

Install

- **TestWise IDE**. Double click *TestWise-Community-4.x-setup.exe* to install, accept all default options. The default installation folder is *C:\agileway\TestWise*. Launch TestWise after the installation completes.

---

[1]http://zhimin.com/books/pwta
[2]http://testwisely.com/testwise/downloads

- **TestWise Recorder**. TestWise comes with a lightweight recorder (a Firefox extension) to record user operations in a Firefox browser into executable test scripts.

  To install, navigate to folder *C:\agileway\TestWise\thirdparty\FireFox_AddOns* (or click the link from Start Page in TestWise), then drag *testwise_recorder.xpi* to an active Firefox Window.

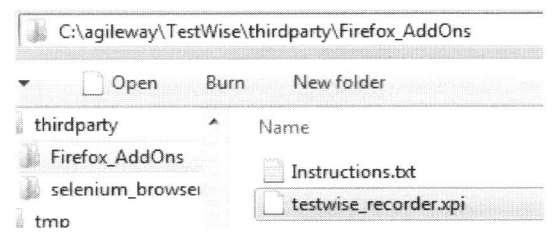

  Locate recorder

  A window with title "Software Installation" will popup from Firefox to confirm installation, click 'Install Now', then restart Firefox.

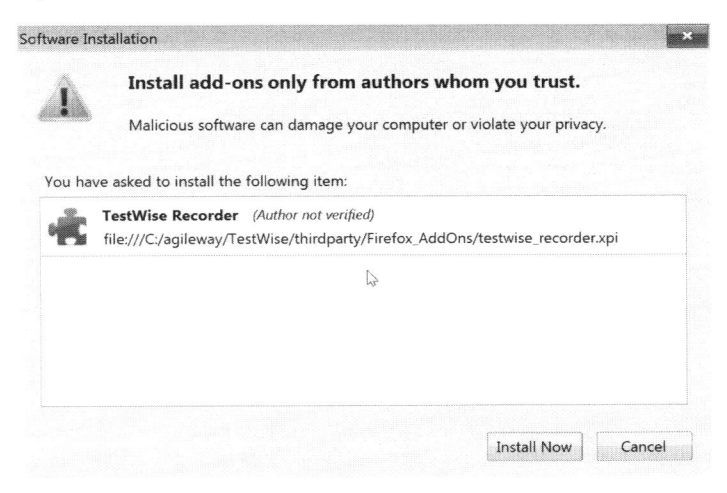

  Install recorder

  In Firefox, select menu 'Tools' → 'TestWise Recorder Sidebar' to enable recording.

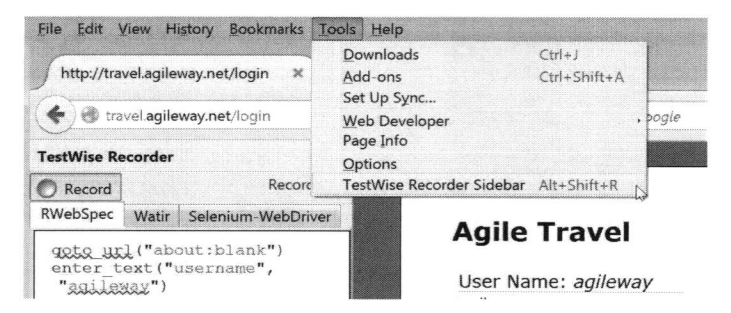

Enable recorder

Create a Test

Now we are ready to create the test for our requirement: "User can login the site". Hope you still remember the test design steps and test data.

Create New Test Project

TestWise has a project structure to organize test scripts. That structure is simply a folder containing all test related files such as test scripts and test data.

As we start from scratch, we need to create a new project first. If a sample project is already opened in TestWise, we need to close it. Select menu File → New Project, which will bring up the window shown below.

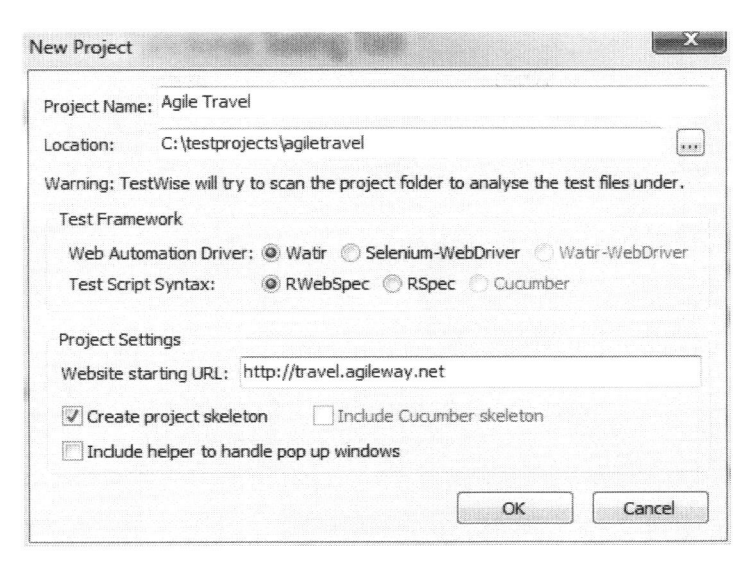

Create Project

Enter project name, project folder and URL of web site to be tested. In this case, we enter "Agile Travel", "C:\testprojects\AgileTravel" and "http://travel.agileway.net" respectively, and then click 'OK' button. TestWise will create the project with skeleton files created for you.

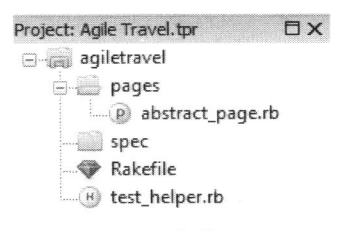

Project Skeleton

Create Test Script File

Now create the test script file for our test. Select 'File' → 'New File',

First Automated Test

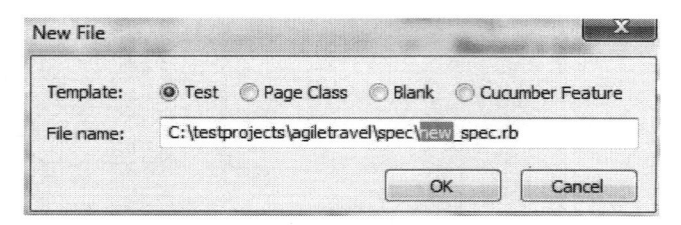

New test

Type text 'login' and press Enter to create new test script file: *login_spec.rb*

Tip: Try naming the test script file something related to the requirement, so you can find it easily later.

A new editor tab is created and opened with a test skeleton:

```
load File.dirname(__FILE__) + '/../test_helper.rb'

test_suite "Test Suite" do
    include TestHelper

    before(:all) do
        # open_browser will try reuse existing IE window if possible
        open_browser(:browser => browser_type)
    end

    after(:all) do
        close_browser unless debugging?
    end

    test_case "New Test Case" do
        # Test Steps go here
    end

end
```

Login test

Recording

Open the site URL *http://travel.agileway.net* in Firefox and enable 'TestWise Recorder SideBar'. Perform the test steps below manually:

1. Enter username 'agileway'
2. Enter password 'testwise'

3. Click 'Sign In' button
4. To add verification for text 'Welcome agileway', highlight the text in browser, right click and select 'Add verify Text for 'Welcome agileway'.
5. Click Sign off link

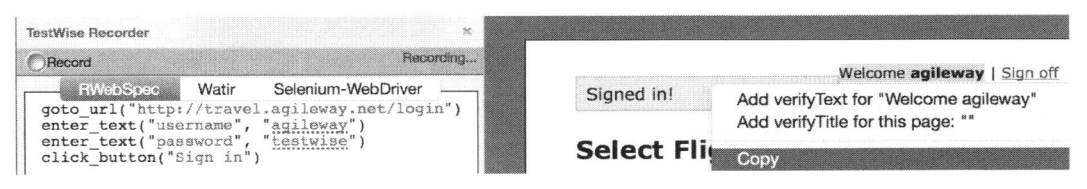

Recording

Test steps are recorded along the way. Once done, inside the TestWise Recorder window, right click and select 'Copy all' to clipboard. If you see the test step *goto_url("about:blank")* (that step tells where the current URL is, we don't need for this case), delete it.

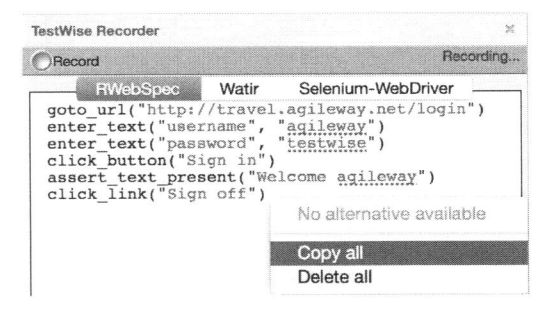

Recorder copying test steps

Create Test Case From Recorded Test Steps

Switch to the TestWise IDE (the *login_spec.rb* editor tab shall be still active), paste recorded test scripts into the test case.

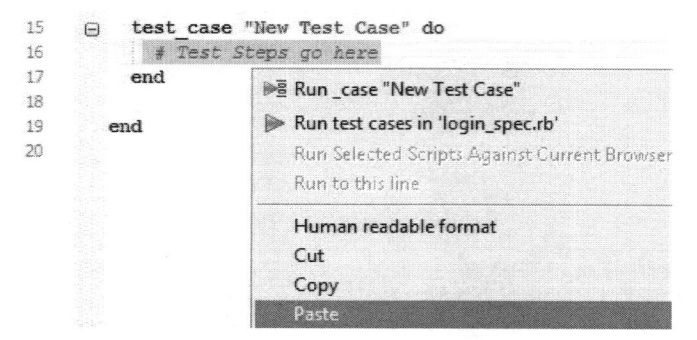

Paste test steps

The test case is created, while we are here, update the test case's name to "User can login with valid user name and password".

Run test in IE

Press ▶ on the toolbar (highlighted in the screenshot below) to run the test case, and you can watch the test execution in an Internet Explorer window.

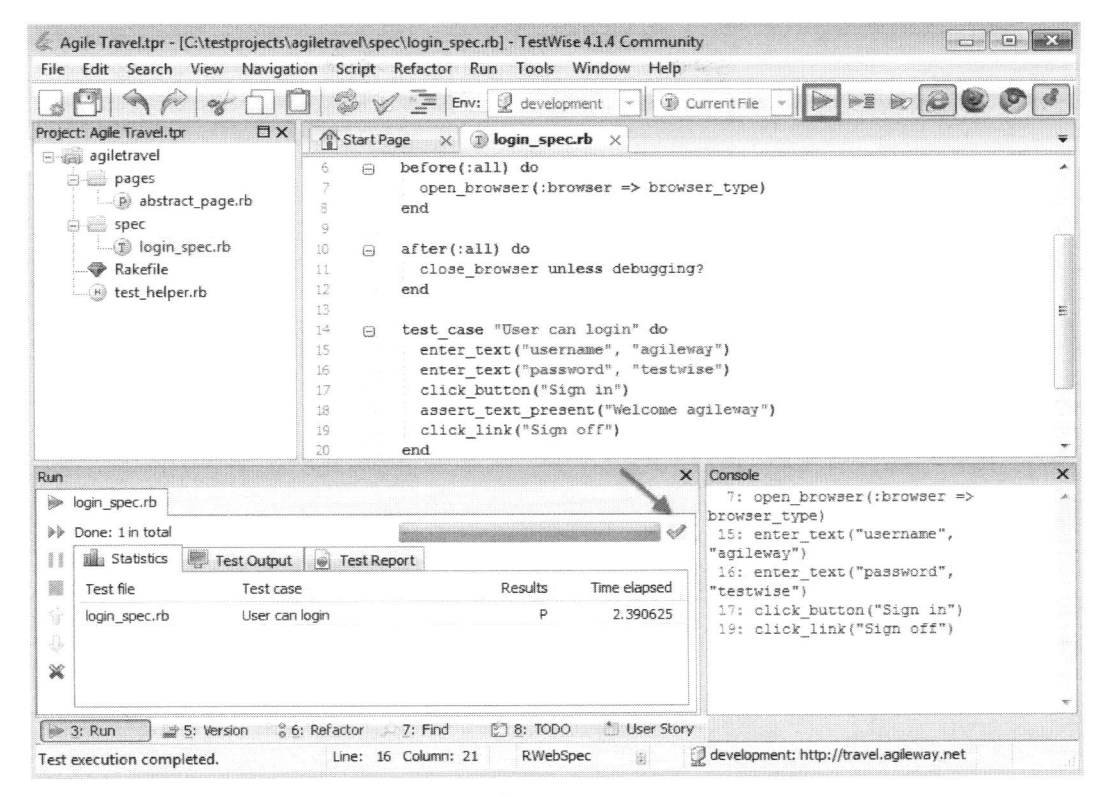

TestWise run

The green tick means the test passed.

When a test failed...

We just saw a successful automated test. Naturally, you will ask what will happen when a test fails? As a matter of fact, during development of an automated test script, we are more likely to get errors or failures before we get it right. It is up to the technical testers to analyse the cause: is it a real application error or incorrect test scripts?

Next, we will make a simple change to the above test script to make it fail:

```
enter_text("password", "invalid")  # now can't log in
```

Click ▶ to run the test. As expected, the test failed.

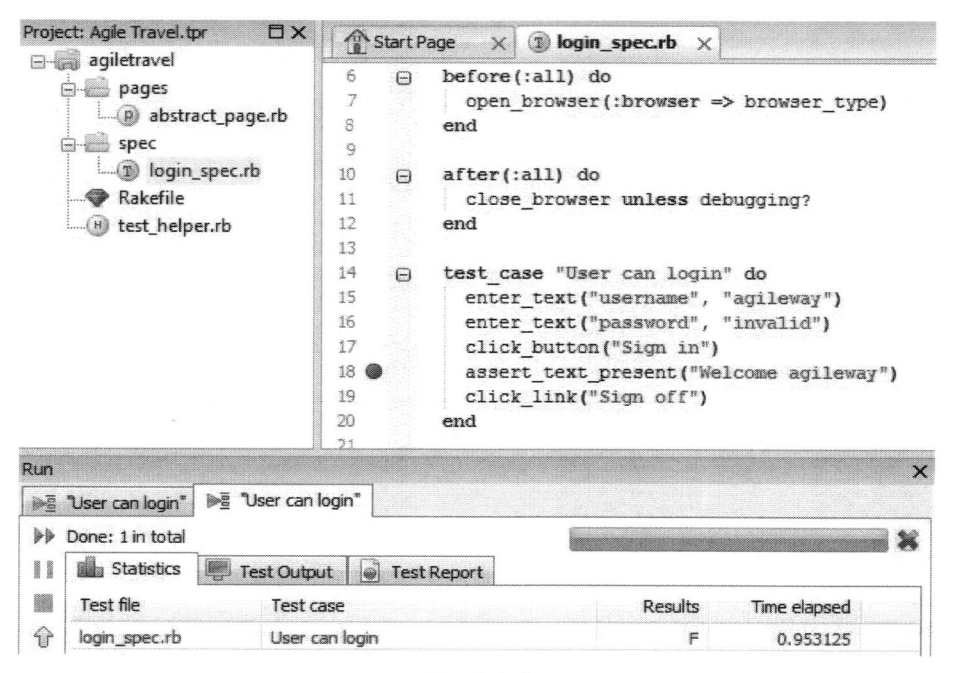

Test failed

In TestWise, the test execution is marked as "Failed" and ● is shown on line 18 of the test script indicating where the failure is.

We, as human, knew the reason for this failure: a wrong password was provided. From the test script's "point of view", it failed due to this assertion not met: finding the text "Welcome agileway" on the page.

If you want to find more details about the cause for test failure, check the text output of test execution including error trace under "Test Output" tab.

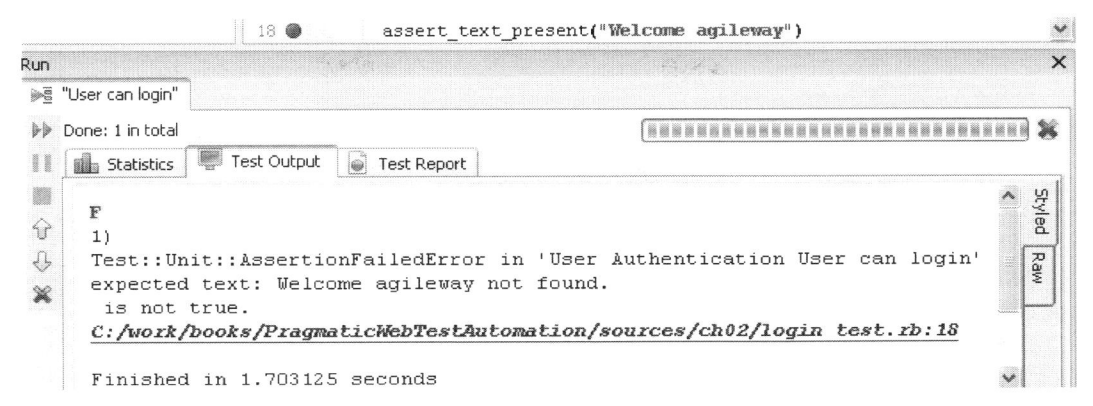

Failed in IE

Wrap up

Let's review what we have done in this chapter. Besides test design, we

- Installed TestWise IDE
- Installed TestWise Recorder
- Created a test project in TestWise IDE
- Recorded test scripts using TestWise Recorder in Firefox
- Created test script from pasted test steps
- Ran test case in IE (pass and failed)

Hopefully you were able to do all that within 10 minutes! You can view the screencast for this exercise online at the book's website at http://zhimin.com/books/pwta[3].

---
[3] http://zhimin.com/books/pwta

3. How Automated Testing works

In the previous chapter, we created an automated functional test running in a web browser, Internet Explorer. This was done by simulating a user interacting with the browser: typing texts and clicking buttons.

Before we move on, let us examine our test targets - web applications (or websites). Simply speaking, a web site consists of many web pages. Behind each web page there is an HTML (HyperText Markup Language) file. Browsers download the html files and render them.

HTML defines a set of standard web controls (aka elements) we all are familiar with, such as text boxes, hyperlinks, buttons, checkboxes, etc. For web application testing, we interact with these controls as well as the text that get marked up in the HTML such as labels and headings.

Now let us review the test script we created in the last exercise:

```
                                          Story ID: User Story/TestCase
test_case "[01] User can login" do
  open_browser "http://travel.agileway.net"
  text_field(:name,"userName").set "agileway"
  enter_text("password", "test")
  click_button("Sign In")                 Steps
  page_text.should contain("Welcome agileway")
end                                       Check
# next test, comments start with '#'
```

Within a test case, test steps can be classified into the following two categories:

- **Operation** (also called step). Performing some kind of keyboard or mouse action on a web page. The above example test has three operations:

  ```
  enter_text("userName", "agileway")
  enter_text("password", "testwise")
  click_button("Sign In")
  ```

- **Check** (also called assertion). Verifying the web page meets the requirement.

```
expect(page_text).to include("Welcome agileway")
```

Web Test Drivers

Web test drivers enable web controls to be driven by test scripts with a certain syntax, for testing purposes. All web test drivers covered in this book are free and open-source.

Watir

Watir (Web Application Testing in Ruby) is a free and open source library for automated testing web applications in Internet Explorer. As its name suggests, test scripts actually are Ruby scripts, a growing popular programming language with *"an elegant syntax that is natural to read and easy to write "*[ruby01].

> "Watir is the most compelling alternative [to Fit] for filling the automated acceptance testing need." — Ward Cunningham

Watir was created in 2005 by Bret Pettichord and Paul Rogers, and it is maintained by many other contributors. Inspired by Watir's success, there are clone frameworks in .NET and Java platforms: WatiN and Watij respectively.

Here is a sample Watir test:

```
require "watir"
browser = Watir::Browser.new
browser.goto "http://www.google.com"
browser.text_field(:name, "q").set "Watir IDE"
browser.button(:name, "btnG").click  # "btnG" is the 'Search' button
```

Selenium WebDriver

Selenium was originally created in 2004 by Jason Huggins, who was later joined by his other ThoughtWorks colleagues. Selenium supports all major browsers and tests can be written in many programming languages and run on Windows, Linux and Macintosh platforms.

Selenium 2 is merged with another test framework WebDriver led by Simon Stewart at Google (that's why you see 'selenium-webdriver'), Selenium 2.0 was released in July 2011.

The above test in Selenium:

```
require "selenium-webdriver"
browser = Selenium::WebDriver.for(:firefox)  # or :ie, :chrome
browser.navigate.to "http://www.google.com"
browser.find_element(:name, "q").send_keys "Watir IDE"
browser.find_element(:name, "btnG").click  #"btnG" is the 'Search' button
```

RWebSpec

RWebSpec is a wrapper around Watir and Selenium. It provides an alternative syntax plus some extra goodies. Here is a sample RWebSpec script.

```
require 'rwebspec'
include RWebSpec::Core
open_browser "http://google.com"
enter_text("q", "Watir IDE")
click_button_with_id("gbqfb")
```

One obvious difference from Watir or Selenium is that **RWebSpec test statements are in active voice**. The following two statements in RWebSpec

```
enter_text("q", "watir IDE")
click_button_with_id("gbqfb")
```

are equivalent to

```
browser.text_field(:name, "q").set "watir IDE"
browser.button(:id, "gbqfb").click
```

in Watir.

Many might find the RWebSpec syntax is more concise and easier to read.

You may mix Watir or Selenium test statements in RWebSpec test scripts like below:

```
enter_text("q", "Watir IDE") # RWebSpec
button(:name, "btnG").click # Watir
```

```
browser.find_element(:name, "q").send_keys("Selenium full featured IDE") # S\
elenium
click_button_with_id("gbqfb") # RWebSpec
```

Automated Testing Rhythm

Regardless of which test framework you use, the 'testing rhythm' is the same:

1. Identify a web control
2. Perform operation on the control
3. Go to step 1 until reach a check point
4. Check
5. Go to step 1 until the test ends

Identify Web Controls

To drive controls on a web page, we need to identify them first.

Let's look at this sample web page:

Its HTML source (you can view the HTML source of a web page by right clicking in the web page and selecting "View Page Source"):

```
User name: <input type="text" name="username" size="20"/>
Password: <input type="password" id="pwd_box" name="password" size="20"/>
<input type="submit" id="sign_in_button" value="Sign in"/>
```

Though the username and password appear the same (text box) on the browser, they are quite different in source. Some attributes in HTML tags tell web browsers how to render it, such as size="20" in user name text box. More importantly, application developers use attributes such as "name" (not exclusively) to determine user's input is associated to which control.

We can identify web controls by using these attributes for testing. Here is one way to identify them in Watir:

```
text_field(:name, "username")
text_field(:id, "pwd_box")
button(:value, "Sign in")
```

As you can see, these three test steps use three different attributes for three controls.

Obviously the easiest way to identify web controls is to use a recorder (a tool records user's operation and generate test scripts), if you have one installed. However, in my opinion, it is essential for technical testers to master and be comfortable to do it manually. The reasons are:

- Some test frameworks don't have recorders or have outdated ones
- Recorders might not work for certain circumstances
- Lack of freedom of choosing preferred attribute (for identifying controls)

In modern browsers, it is actually quite easy to identify element attributes (in HTML source) manually:

Internet Explorer: Developer Tools

IE8 (and later version) has built-in developer tools. You can invoke it by pressing F12 key and Ctrl+B in the Developer Tools window to inspect a web control.

24   How Automated Testing works

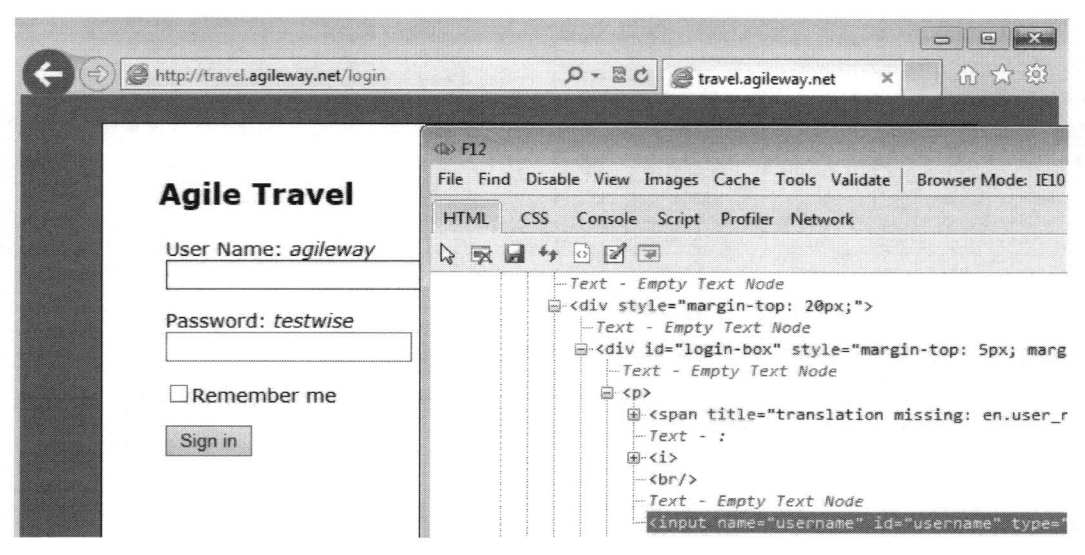

IE Developer Tools

Firefox with Firebug Add-on

Firebug is a popular Firefox extension, one of its feature is to inspect the element's source. Once installed and enabled, right click one control and select "Inspect element".

Firebug add-on

Google Chrome

Google Chrome (and Apple Safari) browser has a built-in support for inspecting web controls.

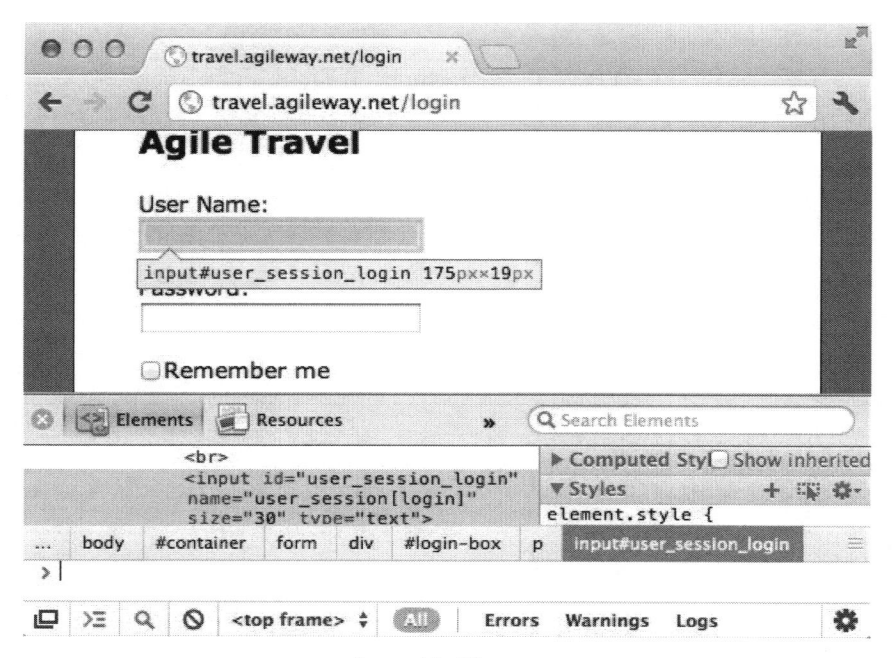

Inspect in Chrome

Drive Web Controls

Once we identify a web control, the next step is to perform required operation with it, such as typing text in a text field, clicking for a button, clearing a checkbox, and so on. Though different test frameworks have different syntax, the idea is the same.

Here are some examples:

Watir:

```
browser.text_field(:name, "user[name]").set "bob"
browser.button(:id, "next_btn").click
```

Selenium:

```
driver.find_element(:name, "user[name]").send_keys "bob"
driver.find_element(:id, "next_btn").click
```

RWebSpec:

```
enter_text("user[name]", "bob")
click_button("Continue")
```

Check

The purpose of testing is to verify a piece of function meeting its purpose. After 'driving' the application to a certain point, we do checks (maybe that's why is called 'checkpoint' in some testing tools).

In the context of web testing, typical checks are:

- verify certain texts are present
- verify certain html fragment are present (different from above, this is to check raw page source)
- verify page title
- verify a link is present
- verify a web control is present or hidden

One key feature of Test frameworks (more in next section) is to provide syntax conventions to perform verifications like the above. Here are some examples:

- RWebSpec

    ```
    assert_link_present_with_text("Continue")
    assert_text_not_present("Server Error")
    expect(page_source).to include("Payment Successful!") # RSpec expect-syntax
    page_title.should == "User Registration" # RSpec should-syntax
    ```

- xUnit (assertion style) with Watir

    ```
    assert browser.html.include?("Payment Successful!")
    assert browser.button(:text, "Choose Watir").enabled?
    assert browser.title == "User Registration"
    ```

- RSpec with Selenium

```
expect(driver.page_source).to include("Payment Successful!")
# RSpec 2 uses be_true, be_false; RSpec 3 uses be_truthy, be_falsey
expect(browser.find_element(:link_text, "Continue").displayed?).to be_truthy
expect(driver.title).to eq("User Registration")
```

Test Frameworks

Web test drivers such as Watir and Selenium drive browsers. However to make effective use of them for testing, we need put them in a test framework which defines test structures and provides assertions (performing checks in test scripts).

xUnit

xUnit (JUnit and its cousins) test frameworks are widely used for unit testing by programmers. xUnit can be used in functional test scripts too, but it is not my preference, as it is not as expressive as the ones below.

RSpec

RSpec is a popular Behaviour Driven Development (BDD) framework in Ruby.

More expressive

Comparing to xUnit test frameworks, RSpec tests are easier to read. For example, for the JUnit test below:

```
class UserAuthenticationTest {
  public void testCanLoginWithValidUsernameAndPassword {
    // ...
  }
  public void testAccessDeniedForInvalidPassword() {
    // ...
  }
}
```

Its RSpec version will be like this:

```ruby
describe "User Authentication" do
  it "User can login with valid login and password" do
    #  ...
  end

  it "Access denied for invalid password" do
    #...
  end
end
```

Execution Hooks

Execution hooks are similar to `setUp()` and `tearDown()` functions in JUnit. Test steps inside a execution hook are run before or after test cases depending on the nature of the hook. The example below shows the order of execution in RSpec:

```ruby
describe "Execution Order Demo" do
  include RWebSpec::RSpecHelper

  before(:all) do
    puts "Calling before(:all)"
  end

  before(:each) do
    puts "  Calling before(:each)"
  end

  after(:each) do
    puts "  Calling after(:each)"
  end

  after(:all) do
    puts "Calling after(:all)"
  end

  it "First Test Case" do
    puts "    In First Test Case"
  end
```

```
  it "Second Test Case" do
    puts "    In Second Test Case"
  end

end
```

Output

```
Calling before(:all)
  Calling before(:each)
    In First Test Case
  Calling after(:each)
  Calling before(:each)
    In Second Test Case
  Calling after(:each)
Calling after(:all)
```

What is the use of execution hooks? Let's look at the RWebSpec test script below (RWebSpec extends from RSpec, so we can use **story** or **test_case** as the start of a test case). There are three login related test cases in a single test script file.

```
describe "User Login" do
  include RWebSpec::RSpecHelper

  story "Can login as Registered User" do
    open_browser
    login_as("james", "pass") # login_as is a function defined elsewhere
    expect(page_text).to include("Welcome James")
    logout
    close_browser
  end

  story "Can login as Guest" do
    open_browser
    login_as("guest", "changeme")
    expect(page_text).to include("Login OK")
```

```ruby
    logout
    close browser
  end

  story "Can login as Administrator" do
    open_browser
    login_as("admin", "secret")
    assert_link_present_with_text("Settings")
    logout
    close browser
  end

end
```

By utilizing execution hooks, we can refine these test cases to:

```ruby
describe "User Login" do
  include RWebSpec::RSpecHelper

  before(:all) do
    open_browser
  end

  after(:each) do
    logout
  end

  after(:all) do
    close_browser
  end

  story "Can login as Registered User" do
    login_as("james", "pass")
    expect(page_text).to include("Welcome James")
  end

  story "Can login as Guest" do
    login_as("guest", "changeme")
```

```
    expect(page_text).to include("Login OK")
  end

  story "Can login as Administrator" do
    login_as("admin", "secret")
    assert_link_present_with_text("Settings")
  end

end
```

By utlizing RSpec's *before(:all)*, *after(:each)* and *after(:all)* hooks, this version is not only concise, but more importantly, every test case is now more focused (distinguished from each other) and test scripts are more readable. For readers who are new to RSpec, don't worry, I will cover it more in later chapters.

Cucumber

Cucumber, another relatively new BDD framework in Ruby, is gaining popularity rapidly. To avoid distraction, we will focus on test practices using Watir+RSpec. There will be a dedicated chapter on Cucumber towards the end of this book.

Run Tests From Command Line

In Chapter 2, we created an automated test script using a recorder and ran the test from TestWise.

One advantage of open-source test frameworks such as Watir and Selenium2 is freedom. You can edit the test scripts in any text editor and run them from command line.

You need to install Ruby first, then install RSpec and preferred web test driver and library (called Gem in Ruby). Basic steps are:

- install Ruby interpreter

    Window installer: http://rubyinstaller.org Mac: pre-installed with OS Linux: get from package manager or compile from source
- install RSpec

    > *gem install rspec*

- install test framework gem(s)

    > *gem install watir*

    or

    > *gem install selenium-webdriver*

For windows users, especially the ones who have difficulty installing gems behind a corporate proxy, you may simply download and install free pre-packaged RubyShell (based on Ruby Windows Installer) at *http://testwisely.com/testwise/downloads*.

Once the installation (takes about 1 minute) is complete, we can run a RSpec test from command line. you need to have some knowledge on typing commands in console (called Command on Windows).

To run test cases in a test script file, enter command

```
> rspec google_spec.rb
```

Run multiple test script files in one go:

```
> rspec first_spec.rb  second_spec.rb
```

Run individual test case in a test script file, supply a line number in chosen test case range.

```
> rspec google_spec.rb:30
```

To generate a test report (HTML) after test execution:

```
> rspec -fh google_spec.rb > test_report.html
```

The command syntax is the same for Mac OS X and Linux platforms.

4. TestWise - Functional Testing IDE

In Chapter 2, we wrote a simple automated test case using TestWise, a functional testing Integration Development Environment (IDE). You are free to use any text-based editors/IDEs to develop Watir or Selenium tests, in that case, you can safely skip this chapter. If you want to be more productive with TestWise, then you might find this chapter useful.

Philosophy of TestWise

The Philosophy of TestWise:

- "The Power of Text"
  (inspired from the classic book Pragmatic Programmers)
- "Convention over Configuration"
  (inspired from popular Ruby on Rails framework)
- Simplicity features are there just for testing.

The Power of Text

Unlike some testing tools, the main window of TestWise is a text-based editor, with various testing functions such as test execution, test refactoring, test navigation, etc. The benefits of using plain text (test scripts):

- Use of Source Control system to track revision and compare differences
- Powerful text editing, such as Snippets
- Search and replace, even across multiple files in project scope
- Refactoring (we will cover this in later chapter)
- Easy view or edit using any text editors without dependency on proprietary tool

Convention over Configuration

The principle of "Convention over Configuration" is gaining more acceptance with the success of Ruby on Rails framework. It makes sense for writing automated tests as well.

In the context of testing, with conventions in place, when a tester opens a new test project, she/he should feel comfortable and can get working straight way.

TestWise defines simple conventions for the test project structure, test file naming and page classes, as you will see later in this chapter. This helps communication among team members or seeking help externally when necessary.

Simple

TestWise is designed from the ground up to suit testers, without compromises often found in testing tools that are based on programming IDEs (which are designed for programmers). Every feature in TestWise has one single purpose: a better testing experience.

To make new-to-automation testers more willing to adopt, TestWise is designed to be small (around 13.5MB), easy to install, launch quickly and get you started in minutes.

> ### Next-Generation Functional Testing Tool
>
> In October 2007, The Agile Alliance held a Functional Testing Tools Visioning Workshop to envision the next-generation of functional testing tools: "We are lacking integrated development environments that facilitate things like: refactoring test elements, command completion, incremental syntax validation (based on the domain specific test language), keyboard navigation into the supporting framework code, debugging, etc." [AAFTTVW 07]
>
> TestWise was designed and implemented before the workshop, but shares the same vision.

TestWise Project Structure

The project structure in TestWise is simple.

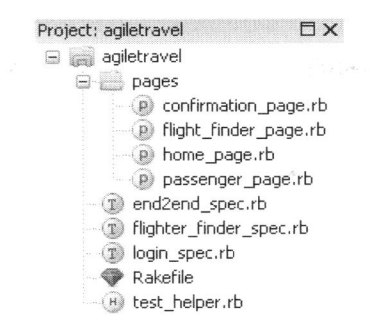

Project structure

There are several file types distinguished by icons in TestWise:

- **Test script files** (xxx_spec.rb)
  One test script file may contain one or more test cases (the extension '.rb' means it is a Ruby script file).
- **Page class files** (xxx_page.rb under /pages folder)
  Page class are for reusable Ruby class representing a web page, we will cover it in detail in the next chapter.
- **Test Helper** (test_helper.rb)
  Common reusable functions are defined in Test Helper. It is included at the beginning of all test script files and the functions are available for all test scripts.
- **Project file** (xxx.tpr)
  Store project settings. To open a TestWise project, look for a xxx.tpr file
- **Rakefile**
  Configuration file for Rake build language (equivalent build.xml in Ant), which can be used to execute all or a custom suite of test cases.
- **Test data** (under /testdata folder, optional)
  The place to put your test data.

Test Execution

Test execution, obviously, is the most important feature for testing tools. TestWise offers several ways to run tests.

Run test cases in a test script file (F10)

A test script file may contain one or more test cases, which commonly form a logic group.

Run individual test case (Shift+F10)

When developing or debugging (trying to find out what went wrong) a new test case, and you just want to run this single test case and prefer to leave the web browser at the state when an error occurred for analyse. And yes, this is the most frequently used method for executing tests.

Run All Tests in folder

Also you can run all tests under a folder.

Run selected tests: Test Suite

A Test Suite is a group of selected test script files to allow a custom set of test cases to be executed together.

Keyboard Navigation

One criteria identified by Agile Alliance work for Next-Gen Functional Testing tools is "keyboard navigation into the supporting framework code". Those used to operating with a mouse all the time might find 'keyboard navigation' is just a matter of personal preference, and wonder how it is made into the list?

For any projects that are doing serious automated testing, there will be a large number of test scripts. When the number is big, being able to find the test case quickly (which at the 'fast end' of spectrum, means via the keyboard), keyboard navigation becomes more than just a convenience.

Go to Test Script File (Ctrl+T)

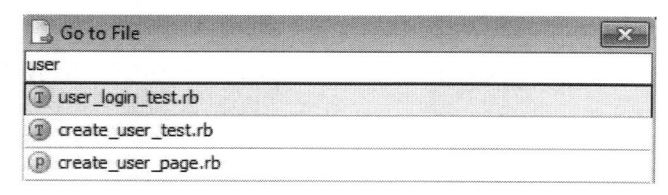

Go to file

Go to Test Case (Ctrl+Shift+T)

Go to test case

> **Rocky's mouse**
>
> Once I worked with a tester nicknamed Rocky who was in his fifties. Despite many doubts, he fell in love with automated testing quickly. He developed RSI (Repetitive Strain Injury, a potentially disabling illness caused by prolonged repetitive hand movements) with his mouse hand. Certainly years of the using computer mice had contributed to that. When we worked together on test cases, I moved the mouse to the far right side and sometimes even put a piece of paper between him and the mouse. Changing a habit is never easy, but Rocky was doing admirably well. Weeks later, Rocky used the keyboard than the mouse and felt more productive as a result. Months later after I left the project, I met one of his colleagues, who told me: he saw Rocky once snapped the mouse on his desk, and said to himself: *"Zhimin said not to use it"*.

Snippets

Snippets in TestWise are small bits of text that expand into full test script statements. The use of snippets helps to create test steps more effectively when crafted manually. For example, type '**cl**' then press Tab key in a script editor, TestWise will expand it into the test statement below (clicking a hyperlink):

cl   `TAB`   click_link("**LINK_TEXT**")

There are two ways to insert a snippet:

1. Enter snippet abbreviation, then press Tab key
2. Press 'Ctrl+J' and select from the list, or type to narrow down the selection.

After a snippet is expanded, you may type over the highlighted text and press Tab to move to next one if there is any. For instance,

```
enter_text("FIELD_NAME", "VALUE")
```

Snippet

type "username" then press Tab key, the test statement becomes:

```
enter_text("username", "VALUE")
```

Snippet: move to next stop

Script Library

For testers who are new to the test framework and do not know the script syntax, may have many 'how-to' questions such as: What is the test script syntax for clicking a button?, How to assert the checkbox is checked?, etc. TestWise's built-in script library can provide the answers.

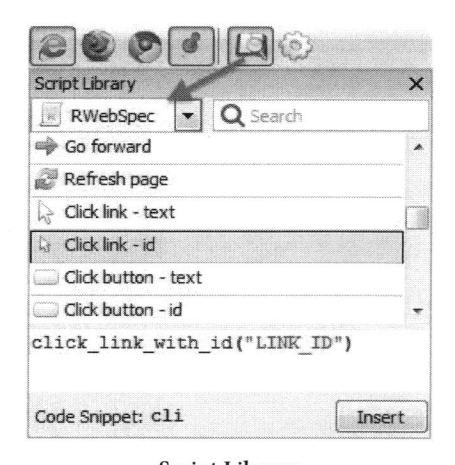

Script Library

Test Refactoring

Test Refactoring is a process of refining test scripts to make it easier to read, and more importantly, easier to maintain. One unique feature of TestWise is its refactoring support, performing test refactoring efficiently and reliably.

We will cover this important topic in later chapters.

Wrap Up

We quickly introduced some features of TestWise to help you develop test scripts more efficiently. For more details, please check TestWise online documentation and screencasts.

5. Case Study

In this chapter, we will write six automated tests for a test web site.

Test Site

In this over-simplified flight booking system: Agile Travel (http://travel.agileway.net[1]), there are 4 high level functions on 4 web pages:

Sign in → Select flights → Enter passenger details → Pay by credit card (then check confirmation)

Some may think the confirmation should have its own page. That's correct, however, I combined the payment page and the confirmation page for testing AJAX.

We are going to write several test cases to verify core functions below:

- Sign in
- Select flights
- Enter passenger details
- Pay by credit card

We will create four test script files, inside which are test cases that are dedicated to testing each core function.

I suggest you spend a few minutes playing with this web site to get familiar to it, as you do for your work.

Preparation

The automated test framework used in this case study are Watir (with RWebSpec extension) + RSpec, and automated tests will be executed in Internet Explorer. (For readers who are more interested in Selenium or running tests against Firefox and Chrome, we will cover in later chapters. I strongly recommend all readers go through this exercise.)

---

[1]http://travel.agileway.net

Web Site: http://travel.agileway.net
Test user login: agileway/testwise
Platform: IE9+ on Windows 7 or later, or Mac
Software to be installed: TestWise IDE (any edition), FireFox with TestWise Recorder plug-in

Create Test Project

Objective

- Create a test project in TestWise

Assume there is an existing folder c:\work\agiletravel, we can add a folder *ui-tests* under it to store our automated test scripts.

In TestWise, select menu 'File' → 'New Project' (close the existing project first if there is one), specify

- name of test project
- test project folder
- select "**Watir**" for web automation driver and "**RWebSpec**" for syntax.
- web site URL

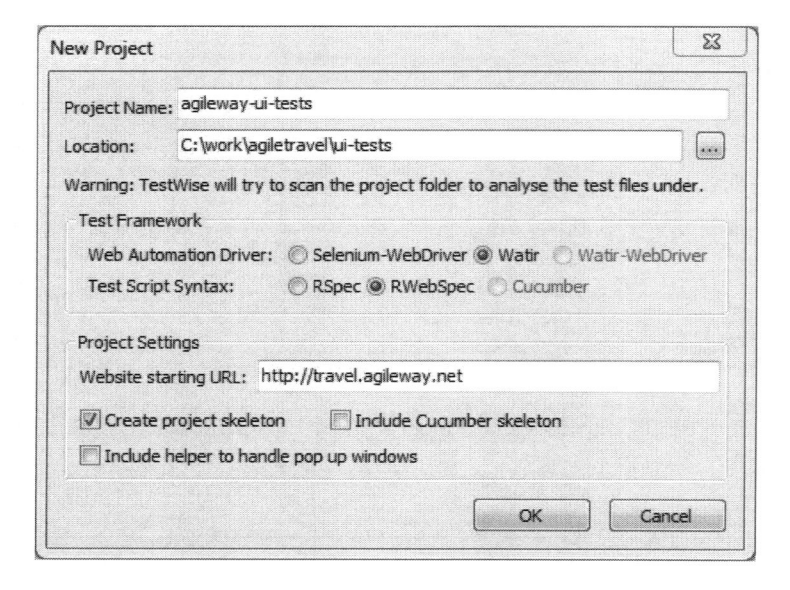

If you want to open this project in TestWise later, select menu 'File' → 'Open Project', locate the project file *agiletravel-ui-tests.tpr* under *c:\work\agiletravel\ui-tests* folder.

Test Suite: Sign in

Objective

- Create test cases using a recorder
- Multiple test cases in same test script file
- Analyse test error
- Understand test execution interference

Test Design

We start with two simple and common test cases: one positive and one negative

- Sign in OK
- Sign in failed with invalid password

Positive Case: User can sign in OK

Select menu 'File' → 'New File', enter file name as 'login_spec.rb'

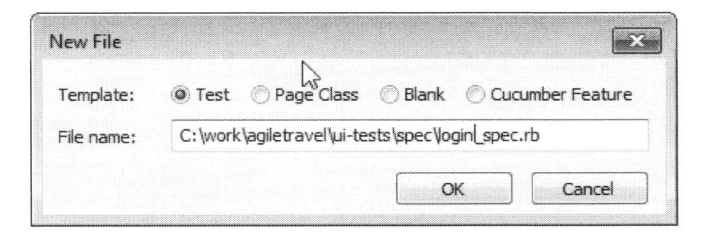

A test case skeleton is created in newly created test script file *login_spec.rb*:

```
test_case "New Test Case" do
  # Test Steps go here
end
```

Set test case name by changing the text "New Test Case" to "User can sign in OK".

Start FireFox browser, navigate to our test site URL: *http://travel.agileway.net*, and enable TestWise Recorder by selecting menu 'Tools' → 'TestWise Recorder Sidebar'. In Firefox, sign in by entering user name and password (*agileway*/*testwise*), and clicking 'Sign in' button.

A test case is not complete without checks. We could use the presence of the text 'Welcome (username)' as the determination of a user is signed in successfully. To create this assertion step, highlight "Welcome XXX" text, right click and select 'Add verifyText for ...'.

Now right click in the recorder window and 'Copy all' recorded test steps:

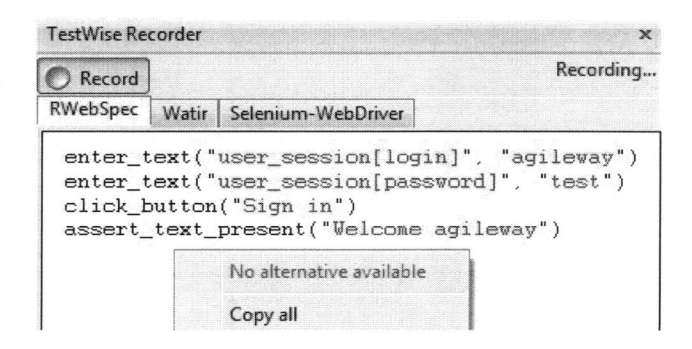

Paste recorded test steps in the test case in TestWise. Now we get:

```
test_case "User can sign in OK" do
  enter_text("username", "agileway")
  enter_text("password", "testwise")
  click_button("Sign in")
  assert_text_present("Welcome agileway")
end
```

Run the test (right click any line within the test case and select *Run "User can sign in OK"*)

```
15      test_case "User can sign in OK" do
16        enter_text("username", "agileway")
17
18        ▶ Run _case "User can sign in OK"        Ctrl+Shift+F10
19        ▶ Run test cases in 'login_spec.rb'     Shift+F10
```

It passed! (indicated by the green tick)

Test file	Test case	Results	Time elapsed
login_spec.rb	User can sign in OK	P	2.25

Negative Case: User failed to sign in due to invalid password

Now we continue to add another login related test case in *login_spec.rb*: user failed to sign in with invalid password. By using TestWise Recorder, we can quickly create this negative test case as below:

```
test_case "User failed to sign in due to invalid password" do
  enter_text("username", "agileway")
  enter_text("password", "bad pass")
  click_button("Sign in")
  assert_text_present("Invalid email or password")
end
```

Run the test and you might get the error below (on line 24):

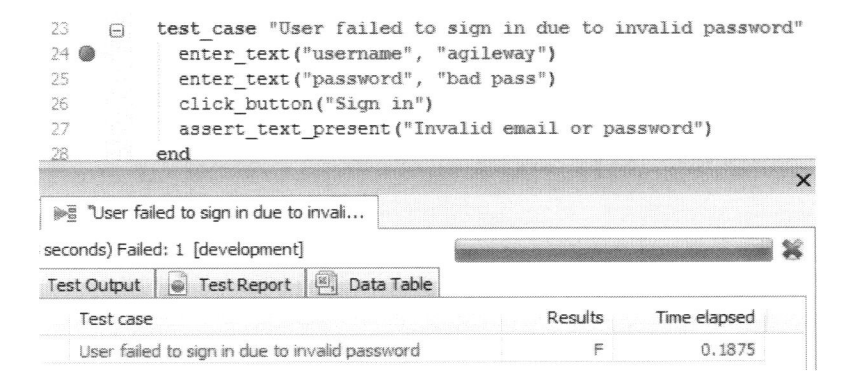

```
23      test_case "User failed to sign in due to invalid password"
24        enter_text("username", "agileway")
25        enter_text("password", "bad pass")
26        click_button("Sign in")
27        assert_text_present("Invalid email or password")
28      end
```

Test case	Results	Time elapsed
User failed to sign in due to invalid password	F	0.1875

48   Case Study

(If you didn't get this error, you probably closed the browser before executing this test)

Clicking the 'Test Output' tab, error trace tells us that the element with name "username" could not be located:

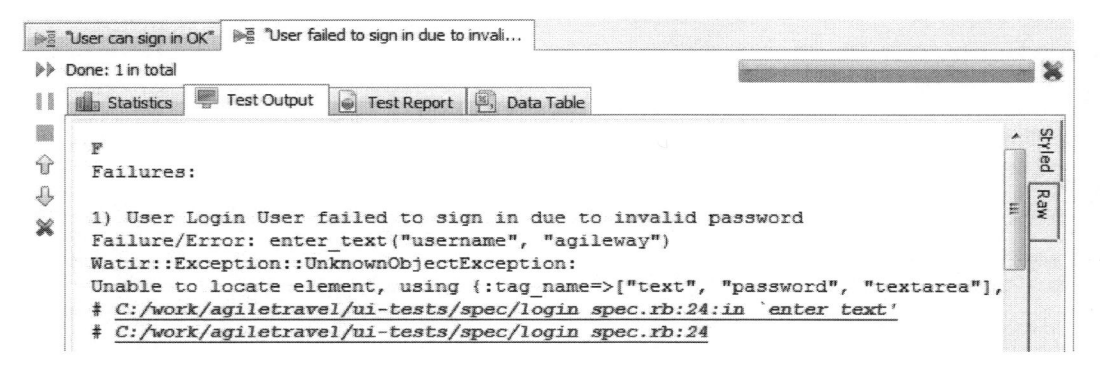

```
F
Failures:

1) User Login User failed to sign in due to invalid password
   Failure/Error: enter_text("username", "agileway")
   Watir::Exception::UnknownObjectException:
   Unable to locate element, using {:tag_name=>["text", "password", "textarea"],
   # C:/work/agiletravel/ui-tests/spec/login_spec.rb:24:in `enter_text'
   # C:/work/agiletravel/ui-tests/spec/login_spec.rb:24
```

Why? If you switch to the Internet Explorer window, the page showing in IE is the one after signing in successfully, as the result of executing the first test case. Our second test case was expecting the home page to enter a user name in a text box. Well, since the current page is not the home page, the test failed.

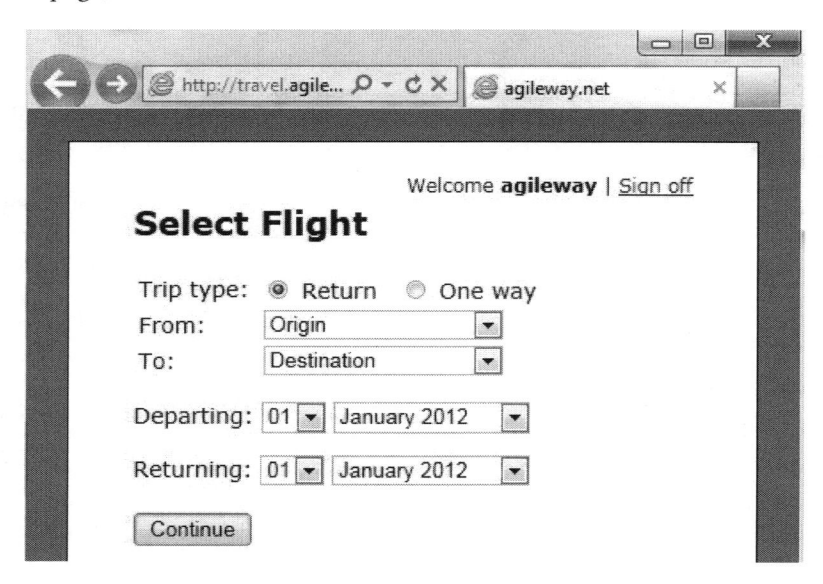

If you close the IE window and run this test case again, it will pass.

How can you prevent execution of the first test case from affecting the second one? One solution is to add a 'sign off' step: `click_link("Sign off")` at the end of the first test case.

```
story "User can sign in OK" do
  enter_text("username", "agileway")
  enter_text("password", "testwise")
  click_button("Sign in")
  assert_text_present("Welcome agileway")
  click_link("Sign off")
end
```

Now Click ▶ on the toolbar to run the two test cases in *login_spec.rb*. Both should pass now.

Test Suite: Select Flights

Objective

- Verify text across pages
- Check dynamic page

Test Case Design

There are quite a few scenarios we could write tests for on this page. For this exercise, we will write just two:

- A return trip
- A one-way trip

Case 1: Return trip

Create a new test script file: *flight_spec.rb*.

```
test_case "Return trip" do
  enter_text("username", "agileway")
  enter_text("password", "testwise")
  click_button("Sign in")
  click_radio_option("tripType", "return")
  select_option("fromPort", "Sydney")
  select_option("toPort", "New York")
  select_option("departDay", "02")
  select_option("departMonth", "May 2012")
  select_option("returnDay", "04")
  select_option("returnMonth", "June 2012")
  click_button("Continue")

  assert_text_present("2012-05-02 Sydney to New York")
  assert_text_present("2012-06-04 New York to Sydney")
end
```

You might notice the step below wasn't included in the recorded test steps.

```
click_radio_option("tripType", "return")
```

This is because this radio button was already pre-selected. You may skip this step. I added this step as I want to make sure this radio button is selected. To record this step, you

- click 'One way' radio button
- right click in the recorder to clear test steps
- click 'Return' radio button

Or you could try inspecting the HTML source manually (see 'Identify Web Controls' section in Chapter 3).

Case 2: One-way trip

Still in *flight_spec.rb*, add the second test case: one-way trip.

```
test_case "One-way trip" do
  enter_text("username", "agileway")
  enter_text("password", "testwise")
  click_button("Sign in")
  click_radio_option("tripType", "oneway")
  select_option("fromPort", "Sydney")
  select_option("toPort", "New York")
  select_option("departDay", "02")
  select_option("departMonth", "May 2012")
  click_button("Continue")

  assert_text_present("2012-05-02 Sydney to New York")
end
```

You may try adding 'sign off' steps to make both the test cases work. But there is another easier and cleaner way.

Technique: Use execution hooks

You might have noticed that both test cases start with same 3 sign-in test steps and end with a sign off test step. If we think about it, we don't have to test the functionality of signing in and signing off for each test case. In fact, our focus is testing the different scenarios after signed in.

With the knowledge of RSpec, we can move these 3 test steps into a '*before(:all)*' execution hook. This way, we only need to sign in once regardless of how many test cases in this test script file.

```
before(:all) do
  open_browser
  enter_text("username", "agileway")
  enter_text("password", "testwise")
  click_button("Sign in")
end

after(:all) do
  close_browser unless debugging?
end
```

```
test_case "Return trip" do
  click_radio_option("tripType", "return")
  # ...
end

test_case "One-way trip" do
  click_radio_option("tripType", "oneway")
  # ...
end
```

If you run the test script file (both test cases), the second test case failed. That's because after execution of first test, the browser has gone to the next page: Passenger Page. To make the second test case (as well the first one) pass, we could use another execution hook: before(:each).

```
before(:each) do
  goto_page("/flights/start") #before each test, make sure on flight page
end
```

Tip: You could use TestWise Snippets to enter this test step: type 'gp' then press 'Tab' key.

There is no need to use the recorder here, just type in the test step (a good test automation specialist may use recorders wisely but won't totally depend on them). The string "/flights/start" is the relative URL of test site, which you can get by examining the address showing in a browser.

Technique: Check Dynamic UI

In the second test case, when we select the one way trip radio button, the return date section is hidden. It is done via JavaScript. How do we check that in automated test scripts? We can inspect the HTML source and review the section containing the return date element. Below is a screenshot of using FireBug in Firefox.

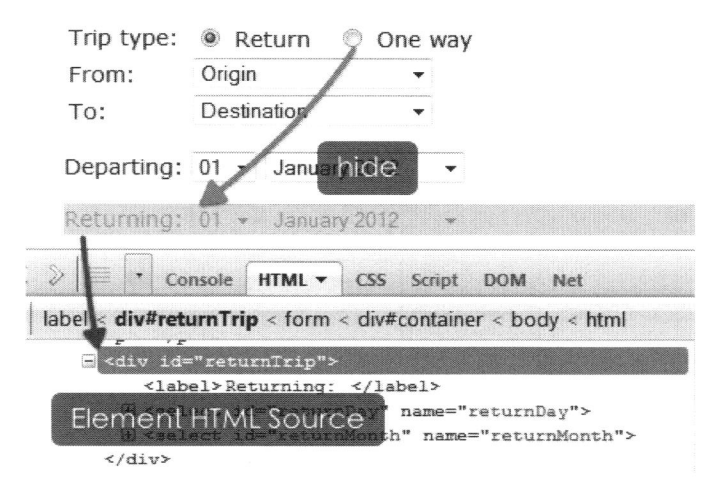

The HTML fragment `<div id="returnTrip">` is the section that will be hidden when the 'One way' radio button is clicked.

Click the script library icon on the toolbar in TestWise, which provides help on finding test or assertion steps. Type in 'hidden' and press 'Enter', we see the assertion statement we need. Navigate the cursor to the right place (after clicking 'oneway' radio button) and press the 'Insert' button, the following statement will be added in the test script editor:

`assert_hidden(:tag, :element_id)`

Update it to:

`assert_hidden(:div, "returnTrip")`

This sounds more complex than it actually is. The screenshot below shows how easy it really is.

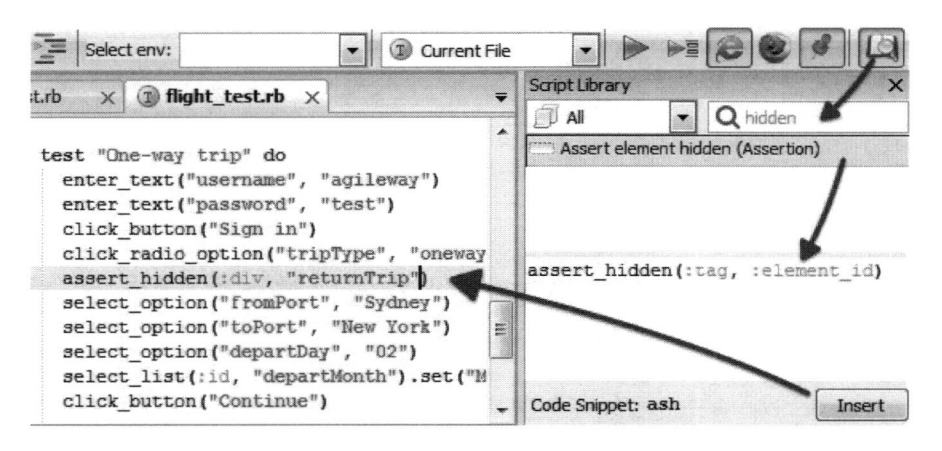

The complete test case:

```
test_case "One-way trip" do
  click_radio_option("tripType", "oneway")
  assert_hidden(:div, "returnTrip")
  select_option("fromPort", "Sydney")
  select_option("toPort", "New York")
  select_option("departDay", "02")
  select_option("departMonth", "May 2012")
  click_button("Continue")

  assert_text_present("2012-05-02 Sydney to New York")
end
```

Enter Passenger Details

Objective

- Validation
- Assert value in a text field
- Use raw Watir test steps

Test Design

For the passenger page, a business rule states that a last name must be provided. We could create a separate test case for each validation, however, this will be an overkill. We can simply add the validation within the main stream test case. That is,

- submit the form without entering last name
- verify the validation error message
- enter first name and last name
- submit the form
- verify the passenger name is saved

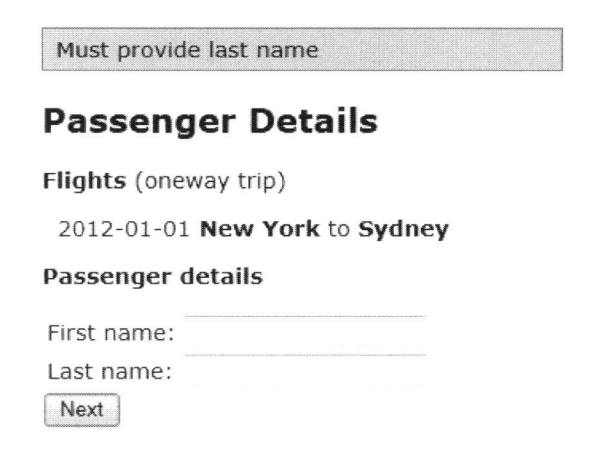

If the passenger details are saved properly, the full name is pre-populated as card holder name on the credit card page. We could use this as our check, i.e. getting value of text box with name "holder_name".

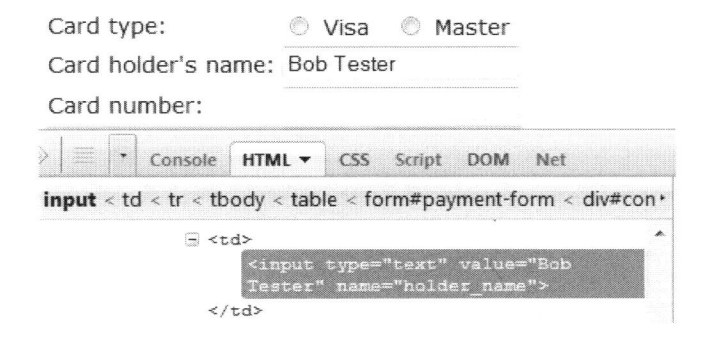

So far the test scripts I have showed are in RWebSpec, an extension of Watir and Selenium WebDriver. However at some point you really need to know the framework underneath, as it provides ultimate flexibility. For this passenger test case, we are going to write it in Watir syntax. Watir test syntax can be directly used in RWebSpec tests.

TestWise recorder records operations in Watir as well. This time, we create the test case from recorded test steps under 'Watir' tab.

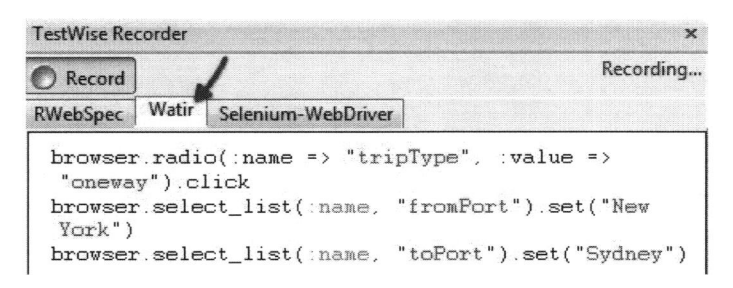

```
TestWise Recorder                                    x
○ Record                                     Recording...
RWebSpec | Watir | Selenium-WebDriver
  browser.radio(:name => "tripType", :value =>
    "oneway").click
  browser.select_list(:name, "fromPort").set("New
    York")
  browser.select_list(:name, "toPort").set("Sydney")
```

Now we get the test case (in Watir):

```
test_case "Can enter passenger details (watir)" do
  # sign in steps in before(:all)
  if RWebSpec.framework =~ /watir/i

    browser.radio(:name => "tripType", :value => "return").click
    browser.select_list(:name, "fromPort").select("New York")
    browser.select_list(:name, "toPort").select("Sydney")
    browser.select_list(:id, "departDay").select("04")
    browser.select_list(:id, "departMonth").select("March 2012")
    browser.select_list(:id, "returnDay").select("07")
    browser.select_list(:id, "returnMonth").select("April 2012")
    browser.button(:value,"Continue").click
    # now on passenger page
    browser.button(:value,"Next").click
    expect(browser.text).to include("Must provide last name")
    browser.text_field(:name, "passengerFirstName").set("Bob")
    browser.text_field(:name, "passengerLastName").set("Tester")
    browser.button(:value,"Next").click

    expect(text_field(:name, "holder_name").value).to eq("Bob Tester")
```

```
    end
end
```

The last assertion step is not from the recorder, you type it in. Also you might have noticed the last test step missed 'browser.'. That's OK, RWebSpec allows that.

For Mac/Linux users, equivalent test script in Selenium-WebDriver:

```
test_case "Can enter passenger details (selenium)" do
  if RWebSpec.framework =~ /selenium/i

    browser.find_elements(:name => "tripType").each { |elem| elem.click && b\
reak if elem.attribute("value") == "return" && elem.attribute("type") == "ra\
dio" }
    Selenium::WebDriver::Support::Select.new(browser.find_element(:name, "fr\
omPort")).select_by(:text, "New York")
    Selenium::WebDriver::Support::Select.new(browser.find_element(:name, "to\
Port")).select_by(:text, "Sydney")
    Selenium::WebDriver::Support::Select.new(browser.find_element(:id, "depa\
rtDay")).select_by(:text, "04")
    Selenium::WebDriver::Support::Select.new(browser.find_element(:id, "depa\
rtMonth")).select_by(:text, "March 2012")
    Selenium::WebDriver::Support::Select.new(browser.find_element(:id, "retu\
rnDay")).select_by(:text, "07")
    Selenium::WebDriver::Support::Select.new(browser.find_element(:id, "retu\
rnMonth")).select_by(:text, "April 2012")
    browser.find_element(:xpath,"//input[@value='Continue']").click

    # now on passenger page
    browser.find_element(:xpath,"//input[@value='Next']").click
    expect(browser.text).to include("Must provide last name")
    browser.find_element(:name, "passengerFirstName").send_keys("Bob")
    browser.find_element(:name, "passengerLastName").send_keys("Tester")
    browser.find_element(:xpath,"//input[@value='Next']").click

    expect(browser.find_element(:name, "holder_name")["value"]).to eq("Bob T\
ester")
  end
end
```

Book confirmation after payment

Objective

- AJAX Testing
- Retrieving text or value from specific element

Test Design

We navigate our way to the payment page. After filling in the credit card details and clicking on the 'Pay now' button, an animated loading image (see below) displays indicating that the payment is being processed.

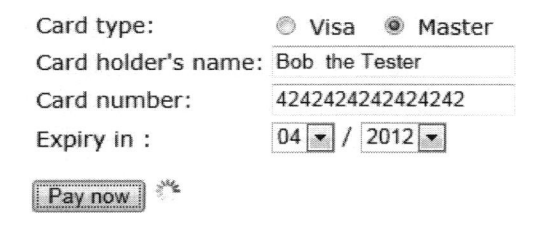

After a few seconds, the flight book confirmation is displayed containing a booking number and flight details. The animated loading image disappears.

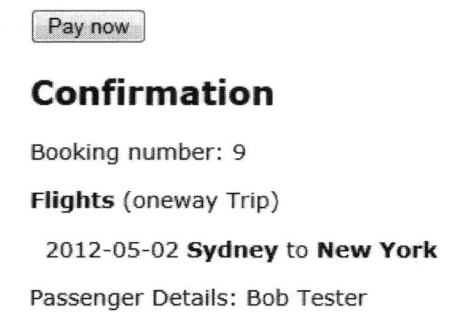

Technique: Testing AJAX

I am sure that you are now quite familiar with this kind of user experience - the web page processes information and shows the results without having to refresh the whole page.

The term used to describe the technology responsible for this enhanced user experience is 'AJAX'. From the testing perspective, an AJAX operation immediately 'completes' after the mouse/keyboard action (such as clicking the 'Pay now' button), no page reload is observed. After the server finished processing the request, seconds or even minutes later, some part of web page may be updated.

One simple solution for testing an AJAX operation is to wait enough time for the AJAX operation to fully complete, then perform assertions like below:

```
click_button("Pay now")
sleep 30 # wait 30 seconds
assert_text_present("Booking number")
```

The above approach works, but is not efficient. If the AJAX operation finishes early, the test execution will still pause there and wait unnecessarily. RWebSpec introduces a convenient function *try_for(seconds) { test steps }* to keep trying next test steps every 1 second up to a specified time. If the operation was performed successfully within the given time, it moves on to the next test step. If the operation still cannot be performed after that time, an error is thrown.

```
try_for(30) { assert_text_present("Booking number")}
```

Technique: Displaying value from specific HTML element in console

Sometimes it may be useful to get a value or text from a specific element on the page. For example, if the booking number in this website is in some number pattern (such as 20120228-123), we can further verify the booking number against the pattern.

During the development of a test case, we often want to seek confirmation by displaying what we returned (also known as printing out). For instance, a tester may want to print to the console the confirmation number from the test output. In TestWise, you can use the *debug* function to display text in the console window, as illustrated below:

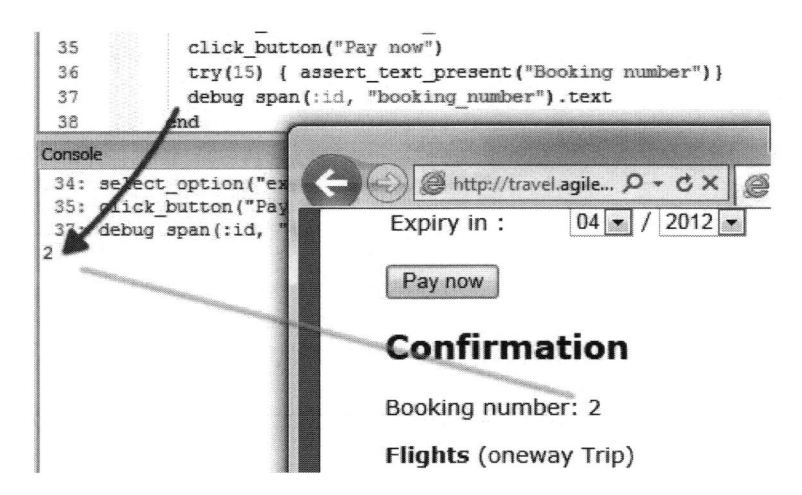

The test scripts for this test case:

```
test_case "Get booking confirmation after payment" do
  # ... up to payment page

  click_radio_option("card_type", "master")
  enter_text("holder_name", "Bob the Tester")
  enter_text("card_number", "4242424242424242")
  select_option("expiry_month", "04")
  select_option("expiry_year", "2012")
  click_button("Pay now")
  try_for(30) { assert_text_present("Booking number") }
  debug span(:id, "booking_number").text
end
```

Run all tests

We can run all these 6 test cases (in 4 test script files) at one go. Right click the project folder and select "Run All in ...". The screenshot below is taken after a successful execution of all 6 test cases.

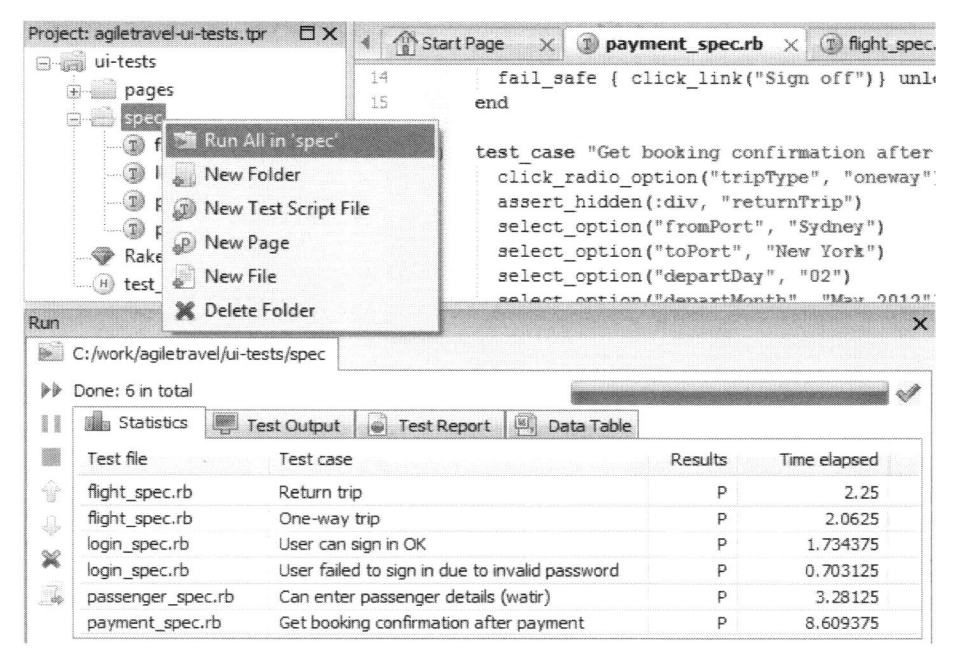

Run all tests

A more detailed test report can be found under 'Test Report' tab.

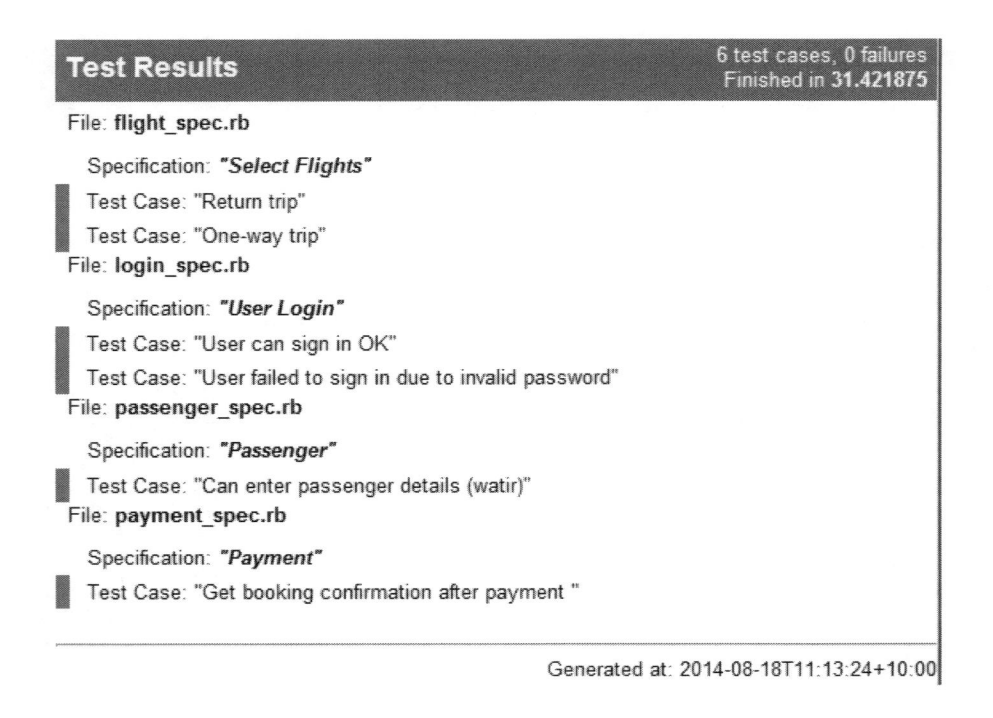

```
Test Results                           6 test cases, 0 failures
                                       Finished in 31.421875

  File: flight_spec.rb

    Specification: "Select Flights"
    Test Case: "Return trip"
    Test Case: "One-way trip"
  File: login_spec.rb

    Specification: "User Login"
    Test Case: "User can sign in OK"
    Test Case: "User failed to sign in due to invalid password"
  File: passenger_spec.rb

    Specification: "Passenger"
    Test Case: "Can enter passenger details (watir)"
  File: payment_spec.rb

    Specification: "Payment"
    Test Case: "Get booking confirmation after payment "

                             Generated at: 2014-08-18T11:13:24+10:00
```

Wrap Up

We have created several automated test cases in RWebSpec/Watir. Along the way, some techniques were introduced. After this exercise, you should be ready to write real tests for your project. I expect that some of you might be very excited, especially after seeing execution of a couple of real tests for your project, and think that test automation is easy.

Here I want to remind you of the test automation camel . After writing dozens of test scripts, you soon will face the first hump: Hard to Maintain. But that's OK. In Chapter 7 and 8, I will show you how to overcome that hump!

After this comparatively long hands-on exercise, we will examine the characteristics of test automation in next chapter.

6. Test Automation Characteristics

I trust that you have written some automated tests with TestWise or your tool of choice. You may have encountered some challenges or difficulties. To better understand automated testing, it is essential to examine the characteristics of test automation.

- Specific
- Clean
- Independent
- Frequent
- Focused
- Programmable
- Creative
- Sustainable

One note before we start: even though these characteristics are listed one by one, they are related to each other.

Specific

This is easy to understand. Automated testing is often associated with the term "Robots". Humans send clear and specific instructions to the robots.

In automated testing, we need to turn each step in test design into clear and specific test instructions in test scripts. For example, to verify a "registered user can sign in successfully" in manual testing is easy; to write this in automated test scripts, we need to think a little further:

How did I know I signed in successfully?
I landed on the home page.
How did I know I was on the home page?
I saw "Welcome XXX" text or 'Sign out' link.

Yes, the above two answers are *specific* and clear test instructions, the test scripts (in RWebSpec) will be:

```
expect(page_text).to include("Welcome Bob")  # test user is Bob
```

or

```
assert_link_present_with_text("Sign out")
```

Clean

Let's start with a question, for the requirement "User can change password", is the design below correct?

1. User logs in with current password
2. User changes the password
3. User logs out
4. Verify the user can log in with new password

Remember your answer. Now if I ask another question: is the design still correct for writing an automated test?

The answer for these two questions is the same: No, one important step is missing.

- Set User's password back to the original one

This step can be executed before Step 1 or after Step 4.

Why? While Steps 1-4 verify the changing password, they also left the system in a non-clean state. What happens if you are asked to perform this test again? Unless the system has a "Reset Database" function built-in, the test will fail from the second execution onwards. To make sure the test executes repeatedly, you have two choices (if not performing the reset step):

- creating a new user with a known password, or
- using the password set by last test if you can remember it

For this simple test, testers will generally act by common sense without realizing this issue when testing it manually. However, if a tester is asked to perform this test often, let's say, twice a day, the issue becomes immediately apparent, not to mention annoying if testing manually.

Writing a *clean* test will not only make the test correct, but also make it a lot easier to develop other tests. The most effective way is to do a system reset before executing each test, that is, the data in application is reset to a known state with a press of button or visiting a special page.

Here is a sample RWebSpec test script (for our password changing test case), calling a helper utility built by programmers to reset the database:

```ruby
before(:each) do
  # call a special URL in application to reset database to its origin state
  goto_page("/reset")
end

story "[8] User can change password" do
  login_as("bob", "test")
  click_link("Profile")
  click_link("Change password")

  password_change_page = expect_page PasswordChangePage
  password_change_page.enter_current("password")
  password_change_page.enter_new("newpass")
  password_change_page.enter_confirm("newpass")
  password_change_page.click_button("Change")

  logout
  login_as("bob", "newpass")
  assert_link_present_with_text("Profile") # login Ok
end
```

> ### The Simpson's Pattern: Reset Database
>
> In a typical Simpsons cartoon episode, Homer might have all sorts of adventures: becoming a millionaire, broke, becoming a boss, fired, ..., etc. However, at the end of

> episode, his situation is set back to where he was at the beginning. This makes it easier for the script writers. Do you see the parallel?
>
> As part of database reset, the records in the database are cleared and filled with pre-defined (or otherwise called seeded) records. A database reset does not only address test data preparation, an important but often overlooked test activity, but also greatly speed up test execution. For example, in a workflow system, a business analyst might take long time to get a record to a certain state. With seeded records via database reset, it now can be as simple as 'reset, go to Record #007'.
>
> It is worth reiterating that the benefits of database resets are to all team members including the programmers and business analysts. Once I asked a business analyst who worked on an application with a database reset facility: "What is the importance of database reset, on a scale of 1 to 10?", he answered "9, no, I mean 10".
>
> Want to see a database reset in action? You can try it out by following the instruction (under Chapter 6) at http://zhimin.com/books/pwta

Implementation of a database reset function is dependant on the technical aspects of the application and software designer's skills. There are two time factors to consider:

- **Design it early, very early**

    It is far easier to implement database reset early. Make it your Iteration 0 task.

- **Make it quick, very quick**

    As database reset is going to be invoked very often, especially by automated tests, we want it to be done quickly, try aiming for an execution time of a couple of seconds. I heard of a large software project trying implement database resets halfway through the development schedule (it surprises me that for almost each project I knew of, the software architects were always too late to realize the needs of database reset). A dedicated team was set up to do it. The best time taken to perform database reset scripts they could achieve was 21 minutes. Not surprisingly, it was not used.

If programmers in your team cannot implement 'Simpsons Pattern' in the application, then testers need to add clean up steps to offset changes made which might impact next runs or other test cases.

Independent

Test cases should be independent from each other, that is, test results are consistent regardless of execution order.

The two cases (in one test script file) below are to test marking a record as 'flagged' and 'unflagged'.

```
before(:all) do
  #...
  create_one_record
end

story "[3] User can flag an item" do
  click_ink("Flag").click
  assert_link_present_with_text("Remove Flag")
  assert_link_not_present_with_text("Flag")
end

story "[4] User can unflag an item" do
  click_ink("Remove Flag").click
  assert_link_present_with_text("Flag")
  assert_link_not_present_with_text("Remove Flag")
end
```

When we run the test script file, both test cases pass. However, if we just run the second test case (TestCase 4) by itself, it failed. Why? It is because Test Case 4 depends on Test Case 3 to be run first, otherwise the record is not flagged, thus there is no 'Remove Flag' link. The same kind of dependency may happen among test script files as well.

From my observation, the opposite scenario are more common, especially for newcomers, that is test cases ran OK individually but failed when ran together. For the two test cases below, a tester started writing the first test case and got it passed. Then she worked on the second and it passed as well. However, when she ran them together (same script file), the second test failed!

```
before(:all) do
  open_browser("http://travel.agileway.net")
end

test_case "Login OK" do
  enter_text("username", "agileway")
  enter_text("password", "testwise")
  click_button("Sign in")
  expect(browser.text).to include("Welcome agileway")
end

test_case "Login failed (incorrect password)" do
  enter_text("username", "agileway")
  enter_text("password", "badpass")
  click_button("Sign in")
  expect(browser.text).to include("Invalid email or password")
end
```

The reason is simple: after execution of first test, the user logs in, the page shown in browser is no longer the home page, which the second test case was expecting to be. To fix this:

```
test_case "Login OK" do
  enter_text("username", "agileway")
  enter_text("password", "testwise")
  click_button("Sign in")
  expect(browser.text).to include("Welcome agileway")
  click_button("Sign off") # back to home page
end
```

Frequent

One key benefit of automated testing is that tests can run frequently. The frequency in test automation has two meanings: needs and outcome.

Frequency as needs

Critical test cases naturally need to be checked often, as those ones are good candidates for automation. Frequently testing the same test cases manually is not only tedious, but also error prone. For example, here is an important test case for an online store system: "When an order is placed, customer shall receive a confirmation email and dispatch department shall receive a work order".

We all know how to check emails, this test is easy to perform manually: set up two test email accounts, open the email client to inspect emails on each account after an order is placed. However, hypothetically, let's say your project is doing daily builds. For this important requirement, your manager asks you to run the test for every build. This will make you think testing differently if you don't want to get bored with tedious work (there could be a lot more tests like this to be done every day). A good reason to automate it, wouldn't you say?

Automated tests are meant to be executed at least once daily or even more often as a part of continuous integration process. We need to take this into consideration when designing automated test cases.

For our sample test case above, here is one solution: with the help from programmers, set up a fake SMTP server and use it for sending emails on test environment (proper SMTP server for the production server, of course), so that every email sent is saved to a specified folder. With that in place, we can change our test design to:

1. Empty files on the email folder
2. Place an order
3. Check the folder, wait up to 10 seconds for two (email) files
4. Open each email file, check Sent From, Subject, Key text in email body

Frequency as outcome

Frequent test executions may result in introducing some unforeseen impact. For example, If a test server is configured to send real emails out, people may get annoyed from receiving a large number of spam emails triggered by execution of automated tests. On one project I was involved, during User Acceptance Testing, suddenly the email stopped working. It turned out that the STMP server flagged the sender email as a spam source after the number of emails sent from exceeded a certain threshold.

Focused

For a given requirement, testers usually create one positive test case (normal path) and several negative test cases (alternative paths). It is not hard to foresee that we are going to end up with many tests if we are doing well (as we all hoped). The quantity of tests may present the automated testers with the problems below:

- Do I cover just one scenario or many scenarios in one test case?
- How to find a test case quickly?
- I want to add new negative scenario for requirement 123, has it already been created?
- For some related test cases, they look very similar, and are hard to distinguish.

So how to organize test cases? Here I share my approach that works well for me.

I group related test cases into a single test script file, like *user_login_spec.rb*. Within one test script file, I identify one web page to test first, write minimum test steps to navigate to the page, then I focus on testing various possible scenarios on this page. Let me explain with an example. A typical online flight booking system works like this:

1. Registered user logs in (optional)
2. Select trip type, date and destination
3. View options and confirm selection
4. Enter/Edit (for registered users) passenger details
5. Payment
6. Confirmation

These six steps match six corresponding web pages, and there may be several test scenarios to be tested on each page:

login_spec.rb	"log in OK", "invalid password"
trip_spec.rb	"one way trip", "return trip", "travel date range check"
flight_selection_spec.rb	"mandatory check", "can view alternative fares by changing dates"
passenger_details.rb	"anonymous must enter passenger details", "registered user details are pre-populated"
payment_spec.rb	"pay by visa card", "pay by master card", "insufficient fund in credit card"
confirmation_spec.rb	"verify passenger details, confirmation code and email"

Test scripts for *trip_spec.rb* (in RWebSpec) may like this:

```ruby
before(:each) do
  enter_text("username", "bob")
  enter_text("password", "testwise")
  click_button("Sign in")
  click_link("Book Flights")
  # Now we are on select trip page
end

test_case "Book one way trip" do
  click_radio_button("trip_type", "oneway")
  #... happy path to a step can verify one way trip booked OK
end

test_case "Book return trip" do
  click_radio_button("trip_type", "return")
  #... happy path to a step can verify return way trip
end

test_case "Travel date range check" do
  select_departure_date("2011-09-20")
  select_return_date("2011-08-20")
  click_radio_button("trip_type", "return")
  #...
end
```

The purpose of this test organizaton is to just focus on scenarios on one application page in a test script file. The theory behind is that if we have one test script file for each web page, most scenarios on all pages will be covered. Also by utilizing the execution hooks like *before(:each)* block in RSpec, we can make the first statement of each test case revealing its purpose. If we examine the 3 test cases in the above example:

```
"Book one way trip"      => click_radio_button("trip_type", "oneway")
"Book return trip"       => click_radio_button("trip_type", "return")
"Travel date range check" => select_departure_date("2011-09-20")
```

We will see the first test steps are the start of testing the business logic of target requirements, not the steps to get there such as user login steps, which reside in *before(:each)* execution hooks. I find this quite handy when maintaining a large number of tests.

Programmable

If I tell you that automated test scripts is related to programming, you probably won't be surprised. Many automated test scripts are in the syntax of programming languages. By utilizing some programming concepts, we can create flexible automated test scripts for performing testing that are otherwise not possible (or very difficult) if done manually.

> **"Programming skills for test automation"**
>
> Programming is the real obstacle of the known 'steep learning curve' of test automation (I exclude those record-n-playback testing tools). It is common that testers are not willing to do automation due to lack of confidence in programming skills. As you see, I touched very lightly on programming, and I believe I haven't lost you yet because you are reading this sentence now. Since you have developed 6 automated tests by the end of Chapter 5, you are the living evidence of the 'smooth learning curve', that is possible.
>
> My take on programming for test automation is to learn as needed, and I think it is wrong to let programming dictates the test scripts. Test scripts are not code, they can be written in a way to be easily accepted by testers. Like the test scripts you have seen using the format of one test statement (line) for one operation (mouse or keyboard or assertion). Once a graduate business analyst learnt how to run and modify automated test scripts just by watching me working for a couple of minutes.
>
> I believe if you put concerns aside, keep reading this book and doing the exercises, you will be fine. There maybe some difficult concepts to master initially, but with the help of Google and the right attitude, it is usually surmountable. Along the way, you are even likely master a certain level of programming . This feedback from a reader: "*I have finished this book and am writing tests for work, WoW! I want to learn more ruby, which book do you recommend?*" is another example of "programming serves test automation", not the other way around.

To illustrate, let's look at this slightly complicated test case: "For a social networking site, system will list a user's potential high school class mates."

Initial Test Design:

1. Create a user 'Bob Tester" who was in "Wisely State High School" in 2003
2. Create a user 'Wendy Tester" who was in "Wisely State High School" in year 2002
3. Login as 'Bob Tester', should see 'Wendy Tester' in potential high school class mate list

Now let's first examine a test log (a log of test execution results) for this test:

```
09-20: {Build.1} Pass
10-05: {Build 2} user 'Bob Tester' and 'Wendy Tester" already in Wisely
       State High, change name to 'Bob1' and 'Wendy1', School to
       'Wisely2 State High", Pass
10-15: {Build 3} Database has been rebuilt, Pass
10-25: {Build 4} change user to 'Bob1', 'Wendy1', school to "Wisely1"
       failed, ..., logged defect #193
10-27: {Build 5} change user to 'Bob2', 'Wendy2', "Wisely2", Pass
```

After every test execution, there will be 2 more users who were in 'Wisely State High' in 2002 added unless database is reset or records are deleted by some mechanism (from my observations, most projects don't have database reset function implemented), and the test data specified in initial test design is not valid any more. From the test log, we can see that the tester in fact has changed the test design to:

1. Create new user 'Bob{X} Tester" with high school class name "Wisely{Y} State High" in year 2000-2003
2. Create new user 'Wendy{X} Tester" with high school class name "Wisely{Y} State High" in year 2002-2004
3. Login as 'Bob{X} Tester', should see 'Wendy{X} Tester' in potential high school class mate list

Now how will you implement this test in automated tests scripts? It is not practical for test scripts to inspect the system for existing users and school names to figure out the value of {X} and {Y}, which is not efficient any way.

I believe many readers have experienced that many test scripts are actually in the syntax of a programming language. The test scripts (except Cucumber Feature files) showed in this book are all valid Ruby scripts. To implement this test case, we could use a programming concept: random number generator to assign a unique name for school name and person names for every test execution.

Most programming languages have built-in function to generate a random number.

```
>rand(100)
=> 77
rand(100)
=> 53
```

We can extend it further to generate character and strings (RWebSpec):

```
random_char
=> "y"
random_str(10)
=> "ybgolqnqqu"
random_str(10)
=> "ivwnzygwef"
```

With this knowledge, we change the test design for automation to:

1. Create a unique high school name
2. Create a unique first user name
3. Create a unique second user name
4. Register first user with the high school name in year 2000-2003
5. Register second user with the high school name in year 2002-2004
6. Login as first user
7. Verify second user in potential high school class mate list

The test scripts (in RWebSpec) will be:

```
test_case "System lists potential high school classmates" do
  high_school_name = random_str(10) + " State High School"
  user1_first_name = random_str(10)
  user1_last_name  = random_str(10)

  click_link("Register User")
  enter_test("username", user1_first_name)
  enter_text("first_name", user1_first_name)
  enter_text("last_name", user1_last_name)
  enter_text("high_school", high_school_name)
```

```
  #...
  click_link("Register User")
  user2_first_name = random_str(10)
  user2_last_name  = random_str(10)
  enter_text("first_name", user2_first_name)
    ...
  login_as(user1_first_name)
  click_link("High School Classmates")
  # saw one class mate: user2
  assert_text_present(user2_first_name + " " + user2_last_name)
end
```

Note: In the above example, we use randomly generated strings (10 characters long) for school and person names. Although absolute uniqueness is not guaranteed, the chances of you getting duplicated names are very slim.

Creative

For test case: "User can reset password", its design may be like this:

1. On forgot password page, user enters a valid email, then submit
2. Wait for the reset email to arrive in an email client
3. Click the reset link
4. Enter new password
5. Login with new password
6. Reset the original password back

To automate this test case, the main challenge is to get the reset link in the email

- the email delivery is usually quick but the delay is unknown
- identification of the correct email in Email client
- extract reset link out from the email

There are tools that can manipulate Outlook actions. But there is a simpler and more reliable way if programmers are willing to offer some help. Programmers can add a bit of code to display the reset link on the web page (see below) straight after user requested a password reset. Naturally, this function is only available on test server, make sure it is disabled for the production server!

> Email sent with password reset instructions.
> /password_resets/xYY52_OlnQgUzNAA7MrJLg==/edit

The HTML source for this fragment is

```
<div id="flash_testwise">/password_resets/1QEEWHNnWh2XqFgH43V48g==/edit</div>
```

Then test scripts can pick up the link from page source, and navigate to it to set new password.

```
reset_link_relative_url = div(:id, "flash_testwise").text
goto_page(reset_link_relative_url)
```

Some may point out that this approach does not test the email actually containing the link. The observation is correct. This can be complemented by checking reset email manually before major builds.

Sustainable

This applies to the automated testing approach as a whole, I list it here because it can be a trap for new players, read on. Quite often I have seen testers get excited after tutorials/training and rush to write a long list of empty test cases as below:

- Registration: can register with correct email and password successfully
- Registration: email has to be valid format
- Registration: email hasn't been taken
- Registration: password must be 6 characters or above
- Registration: password must contain one digit or one upper case character
- Registration: password and confirmation must match
- ....

These are good and valid test scenarios. Nothing wrong with that. As a matter of fact, it shows the tester has done a good deal of thinking.

I am against the approach of creating a list of possible scenarios as place holders without actual executable test steps. Before I explain my reasons, I will tell you how I do it:

1. Identify one test scenario
2. Develop a test case for the scenario, with test steps
3. Get the test running as expected (here I mean test execution not test results)
4. Make sure all existing test cases run OK
5. Repeat Step 1

Now here are my reasons. Firstly, it is impossible to test every possible scenario, this is a fact. We cannot do it with manual testing, nor with automated testing. This means our automated tests are going to be selective. It is OK to list all test scenarios as part of planning exercise, but creating empty test cases is not a good practice. Let's say there are 300 empty test cases with scenarios defined. When you run them, whether you set empty test cases default to pass or fail, it won't be a real reflection of actual application. Furthermore, it gives testers unnecessary pressure when working on test scripts, 'still 297 left, …'.

More importantly, this approach ignores or does not realize that test maintenance usually takes more effort than test creation. It is quite common that a fair percentage of your previously working tests will fail on the next build of the application. It could be due to text changes, business rule changes or real defects. As Test Analysts, it is up to us to analyse and find out the real cause, and update test scripts as necessary. It happens to manual testing as well. As checking is far more restrictive in automated test scripts, more maintenance effort is required. Also, don't forget that more test cases mean longer execution time, and therefore are harder to maintain.

In summary, sustainable test automation means keep existing test cases healthy before writing a new one.

Wrap Up

This has been a long chapter. If you don't remember all the characteristics, don't worry. You can revisit them when you face challenges, some characteristics might make more sense to you then. For now, make sure you understand 'Specific' and 'Clean' well.

7. Maintainable Functional Test Design

"Change is nature, Dad." - Remy, "Ratatouille"

Once I asked a friend whose project recently purchased an expensive automated testing tool: "Assume your web site has 100 web pages, and you have 100 automated test cases generated by a recorder. Now a programmer made two simple changes to web application such as hyperlink 'A' → 'B' on the second page and button 'OK' to 'Continue' on the 13th page, what will you do then?" After a long pause, he answered: "Probably record again".

As all testers who have test automation experience would know an application change may break many automated test scripts, and these kind of application changes happen a lot. To effectively deal with it, testers need to be in a position to respond to a simple application change in a matter of seconds (here I mean the time taken to modify the test scripts). In this chapter, I will show you how.

Record/Playback Leads to Unmaintainable Test Scripts

"Record/playback scripts are notoriously costly from a maintenance perspective." - Lisa Crispin & Janet Gregory, 'Agile Testing'

Some testers think automated software testing through UI is just record/playback, which is very wrong. Why? Recorded test scripts often end up being unmaintainable. There is no doubt that the use of recorders (typically found in commercial vendor testing tools) makes it easy to create test scripts. However, it does come at a cost unless you only run the test once or your application never changes. As the old saying goes: if it's too good to be true, it probably is.

Tool vendors often emphasize how easy it is to create automated test scripts with a recorder. But they don't tell you that the real hard challenge of test automation is to maintain the test scripts along with a frequently changing application. Naturally simple, concise and easy-to-read test script syntax is not rated high in these vendor's list as recorders generate them. Users initially use the tool's playback function to run tests, so they care less about the test scripts as well. This approach might work for a very short 'honeymoon' period, then there comes some application changes, and many if not all test scripts fail to run. Then testers probably record the test scripts again or start to change the test scripts manually. It usually does not take a few iterations for testers to realise this approach is too hard. There are plenty of this kind of stories around. Unfortunately many discontinue with automated testing because of this experience.

You may say, "Hang on, what you showed in Chapter 2 was just another use of a recorder." That's correct. However we aren't finished there. There is another important step missing: refining recorded test scripts into a maintainable format.

Record, Refine, Run

On the Watir forum, you may have seen some advanced Watir users were against the use of recorders. In reality, however, using recorders is probably the best way to get new testers started in test automation. Recorders do provide benefits to testers (new and experienced), if used wisely.

Recording itself is not wrong, it is the way how they are used that is often wrong. In my opinion, if a recorder is used, "Record $\Rightarrow$ Playback" should be changed to "Record $\Rightarrow$ Refine $\Rightarrow$ Run". The 'Refine' step in 'Record -> Refine -> Run' is the process of changing the recorded test scripts into a maintainable form.

Success Criteria

> "Expensive Tools Do Not Produce Better Designs" - The Pragmatic Programmer book, Tip 59

The key to test maintenance (a common problem in test automation) is the test script, not the test tool. Tools vendors like to focus on their tools or deliberately blur the relationship between test scripts and testing tools, often for the sake of commercial interests. Good testing tools should help testers create and maintain test scripts efficiently.

To be able to maintain a large number of automated test scripts that can keep up with application changes, we need to design our test scripts that are intuitive and can be updated efficiently by the tester.

Intuitive to read

Generally speaking, testers are not tech-savvy. Therefore test scripts must be intuitive and ideally readable. How intuitive should (or can) test scripts be? If we step outside testing world, consider how people talk about web sites, you might hear instructions like this:

1. After login
2. you shall see an account summary page
3. on that page, click 'select pay by credit card'
4. Enter your credit card details on payment page
5. Record the receipt number on the confirmation page

This sets a good target for our test scripts syntax.

Easy to Update

The core reason of hard-to-maintain test scripts is **duplication**. It is very similar to the problems caused when software code is duplicated (often by copy-and-paste) in an application. It happens too often when there are changes needed and people forget to update all the references. In the context of test scripts, duplications are often widespread in the recorded test steps. When applications change frequently (almost invariably), duplication will lead to maintenance difficulties.

You might have heard the term "DRY". DRY stands for Don't Repeat Yourself, that is, "Every piece of knowledge must have a single, unambiguous, authoritative representation within a system [Hunt & Thomas 00]". DRY in test automation means if one test step's corresponding operation changed in a web application (such as the button 'Confirm' on the payment page being renamed to 'Pay now'), it is only needed to be updated at one place, regardless of this test step being used by many test cases.

Maintainable Automated Test Design

Let's revisit the sample instruction of how people talk about the use of web sites:

1. After **login**
2. you shall see *account summary page*

3. on that *page*, click 'select pay by credit card'
4. Enter your credit card details on *payment page*
5. Record the receipt number on *confirmation page*

You might have noticed I highlighted the **login** and several *XXX page*s, which are examples of two key concepts for maintainable test design: reusable function and page object.

Reusable Function

As we know, a user login function is commonly consisted of three steps:

1. Enter user name in a text box
2. Enter password in a password box
3. Click 'Log in' button

For this frequently used function, we prefer not to repeat these 3 test steps every single time (which would be a good example of causing duplication) in our test scripts.

Here is a sample test script using a reusable function for login.

```
login("bob", "pass")
# ...
login("wendy", "boss")
```

The function's definition (in RWebSpec):

```
def login(username, password)
  enter_text("user[name]", username)
  enter_text("user[password]", password)
  click_button("Log in")
end
```

Page Object

> "If you have WebDriver APIs in your test methods, You're Doing It Wrong" - Simon Stewart, lead of Selenium WebDriver project.

A web page can be seen as a group of related operations to perform on a single page with one purpose. For example, on a credit card payment page, a user can perform the following six operations:

1. select card type
2. enter text in card holder's name text box
3. enter text in card number text box
4. select card expiry month
5. select card expiry year
6. click 'Continue' button

These six operations on the web page allow users to submit a credit card details to the system.

Web pages not only provide contexts of grouped operations, but also provide contexts for referring information on web sites. For example, if a programmer says "I changed the 'Submit' button to 'Sign up'", others may ask "On what page?". If he said "I changed the 'Submit' button on the conference registration page to 'Sign up'", people would understand.

Page Object is a common test design pattern that groups a web page's operations into a 'logic page object' (feel confused? Stay with me, it will become clear after you see some examples). Here is a sample test script using a page object **credit_card_page**:

```
credit_card_page.enter_holder_name("John")
credit_card_page.enter_card_number("4242424242424242")
# ...
```

The page name *credit_card_page* reveals the purpose of operations on the page, *enter_holder_name* and *enter_card_name are* two operations on this page.

Page Object can be a difficult concept to understand initially. The exercise below should help.

Maintain with Ease

Besides syntax benefits (easy to read), test scripts that make use of reusable functions and Page Objects are much easier to maintain. This is because test steps are now in reusable functions and the operations are in page objects. Test scripts in (top-level) test cases are not referencing test steps directly. Instead it becomes essentially a two tiered arrangement.

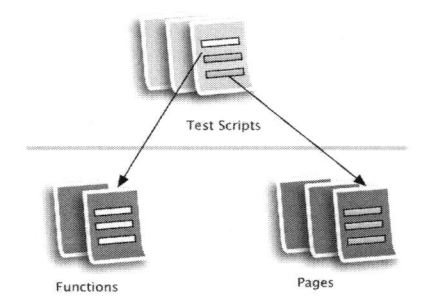

When a change is introduced on a web page, its corresponding test steps need to be updated accordingly. If the affected test steps are used directly in many test cases, we need to update them one by one, which is tedious and error prone. If test cases use page objects, there is only one place that needs to be updated - the functions in the page class. For example, after identifying the credit card page was changed in the new release, we just simply navigate to the definition of page class: *CreditCardPaymentPage* and update the test steps for affected operations there. Depending on the nature of application changes, test cases themselves might not need to be updated at all.

Not convinced? You can watch to see a screencast demonstration: Updating a page class operation to get dozens of affected test cases all passing again, in seconds.

Case Study: Refine Test Scripts

You might have already figured out that reusable functions and page objects make test scripts DRY. Now let's 'DRY' some test scripts.

DRY with Reusable Functions

As usual, we start with an example. Can you identify the duplications in test scripts below?

```
before(:all) do
  open_browser
end

before(:each) do
  goto_page("/")
end

story "Registered user can login" do
  enter_text("userName", "agileway")
  enter_text("password", "testwise")
  click_button("Sign in")
  assert_text_present("Welcome agileway")
  click_link("Sign out")
end

story "Admin user can login" do
  enter_text("userName", "admin")
  enter_text("password", "secret")
  click_button("Sign in")
  assert_link_present_with_text("Administration")
  click_link("Sign out")
end
```

The last steps for above two test cases are the same:

```
click_link("Sign out")
```

As we know, 'user signing out' is a common piece of function which can appear many times in a test project. Let's say, in the next release of application, the programmers change the link text from "Sign out" to "Sign off". What will happen to our test cases? Most of the test cases will fail. How do we get all test scripts to work again? We could do a search-and-replace in hundreds of files, but that may not be the wisest approach.

We can refine our original test scripts by extracting the "sign out" step into a reusable function like below.

```
def sign_out
  click_link("Sign out")
end
```

Then, modify the test cases to use this function:

```
story "Registered user can login" do
  enter_text("userName", "agileway")
  enter_text("password", "testwise")
  click_button("Sign in")
  assert_text_present("Welcome agileway")
  sign_out
end

story "Admin user can login" do
  enter_text("userName", "admin")
  enter_text("password", "secret")
  click_button("Sign in")
  assert_link_present_with_text("Administration")
  sign_out
end
```

Our test scripts now are flexible to cope with this application change. If the 'Sign out' link is changed to 'Sign off', only one update is needed to the function's definition:

```
def sign_out
  click_link("Sign off") # changed in v1.2
end
```

All test cases (regardless of how many of them) still remain intact.

Parameterizing functions

We could improve the above two sample test cases even further. The three test steps below forms a commonly used function: Sign in. Both sample test cases start with the same sign in operation, but with different user name and password.

```
enter_text("userName", "agileway")
enter_text("password", "testwise")
click_button("Sign in")
```

By introducing a function "sign_in_as" with two parameters, we get

```
def sign_in_as(username, password)
  enter_text("userName", username)
  enter_text("password", password)
  click_button("Sign in")
end
```

and update the test cases to use this function:

```
story "Registered user can login" do
  sign_in_as("agileway", "testwise")
  assert_text_present("Welcome agileway")
  sign_out
end

story "Admin user can login" do
  sign_in_as("admin", "secret")
  assert_link_present_with_text("Administration")
  sign_out
end
```

DRY with Page Objects

Only having reusable functions is not enough. When there are too many of them, it will become difficult to remember which function to use or has been used. It is likely that we will end up waiting to write a function with the same name but different functionality on different web pages. It is not too dissimilar to how you need to specify a suburb or city when providing a street address (since there can be more than one street with that name).

Taking the following credit card payment page below as an example, there are two test cases created from recorded test steps:

```
story "First test case: pay using visa card" do
  #...
  click_link("Pay by Credit Card")
  select_option("card_type", "Visa")
  enter_text("card_holder", "John Citizen")
  enter_text("card_number", "4242424242424242")
  select_option("exp_month", "02")
  select_option("exp_year", "2014")
  click_button("Continue")
  click_button("Confirm")
  #...
end

story "Another test case: pay using master card" do
  #...
  click_link("Pay by Credit Card")
  select_option("card_type", "Master")
  enter_text("card_holder", "Joe Public")
  enter_text("card_number", "51234567798746546")
  select_option("exp_month", "07")
  select_option("exp_year", "2017")
  click_button("Continue")
  click_button("Confirm")
  #...
end
```

The above test cases will both work, but will be difficult to maintain. We could extract some or all operations into reusable functions. Unlike the sign-in operation, this payment page is not commonly used (in this application). Also if we keep extracting new functions, we will end up with hundreds of them. Furthermore, when one web page is updated, finding affected functions becomes increasingly difficult.

Here we will use a different approach. We will define a 'logical page' named *CreditCardPaymentPage*, outside of the main test scripts, to represent this credit card web page. As you can see below, it includes six operations and each operation contains a corresponding test step.

```ruby
class CreditCardPaymentPage
  def enter_card_type(card_type)
    select_option("card_type", card_type)
  end

  def enter_holder_name(name)
    enter_text("card_holder", name)
  end

  def enter_card_number(card_number)
    enter_text("card_number", card_number)
  end

  def select_expiry_month(month)
    select_option("exp_month", month)
  end

  def select_expiry_year(year)
    select_option("exp_year", year)
  end

  def click_continue
    click_button("Continue")
  end
end
```

By using this CreditCardPaymentPage, we can modify the test cases to:

```ruby
story "First test case: pay using visa card" do
  # ...
  click_link("Pay by Credit Card")

  credit_card_payment_page = expect_page CreditCardPaymentPage
  credit_card_payment_page.enter_card_type("Visa")
  credit_card_payment_page.enter_holder_name("John Citizen")
  credit_card_payment_page.enter_card_number("4242424242424242")
  credit_card_payment_page.select_month("02")
  credit_card_payment_page.select_year("2014")
```

```
    credit_card_payment_page.click_continue

    # Now on next page
    click_button("Confirm")
    # ...
end

story "Another test case: pay using master card" do
    # ...
    click_link("Pay by Credit Card")

    credit_card_payment_page = expect_page CreditCardPaymentPage
    credit_card_payment_page.enter_card_type("Master")
    credit_card_payment_page.enter_holder_name("Joe Public")
    credit_card_payment_page.enter_card_number("51234567798746546")
    credit_card_payment_page.select_month("07")
    credit_card_payment_page.select_year("2017")
    credit_card_payment_page.click_continue

    # Now on next page
    click_button("Confirm")
    #...
end
```

It reads better, isn't it? Better still, there is another benefit. If one operation on the credit card page is changed in the application (for example, attribute 'card_holder' is renamed to 'card_-holder_name'), how will you update the recorded version of test scripts? How would you do differently for the version using *CreditCardPage*? Probably with a lot of effort. However can you see how much easier it is with our CreditCardPage object?

> **Object Oriented Concept**
>
> The Page Objects pattern is based on Object Oriented (OO) concept. I remember that it took me a long time to understand OO when I was at university (back then I had no tools to try, just theoretical reading from the books). It turned out to be quite simple if it was illustrated with examples. Here is one:
>
> Car is a class, it has following two functions (plus many more...):

> - accelerate
> - brake
>
> My car (the one in my garage) is an object of Car, it can do 'brake' and 'accelerate'. I can physically drive it.
>
> For new automated testers, in my opinion, understanding the above example is probably enough. Deeper knowledge in OO is required for more advanced scripting skills. But don't worry, you will improve with more practice. Now have a think about statements below:
>
> ```
> my_car = Car.new
> my_car.accelerate
> your_camry = Car.new
> your_camry.brake
>
> login_page = LoginPage.new
> login_page.enter_username("bob")
> ```

Wrap Up

Reusable functions and Page objects are two most effective test design patterns to 'DRY' test scripts. They are applicable to almost any test frameworks.

Some readers, especially those who don't have programming background, may feel a bit uneasy about extracting reusable functions and page objects. In next chapter, we will walk through an example of DRYing test scripts step by step by using refactoring support in TestWise.

8. Functional Test Refactoring

In this chapter, I will show you how to apply test refactoring to systematically implement easy-to-maintain automated test scripts.

Code Refactoring

Code refactoring is a "disciplined technique for restructuring an existing body of code, altering its internal structure without changing its external behaviour" ([Fowler et al. 99]). My simplified version of the meaning 'Refactoring': improving the inside but preserving the outside. You probably have heard the term 'refactoring' used by programmers. The rhythm of true refactoring is: "test, small change, test, small change, test, small change. It is that rhythm that allows refactoring to move quickly and safely" ([Fowler et al. 99]). Code refactoring is built on solid unit testing. Without it, programmers are just changing code albeit with good intentions and calling it "Refactoring".

Functional Test Refactoring

Just like programmers source code, test scripts need continuous improvement to make them easy to read and maintain. Many automation testers develop an automated test script (after test design) using an approach like this: record test steps with a recorder or enter test steps manually, run it, make necessary changes to get it running as expected in browser. However, the job is not done unless you never need to run that test ever again. Test cases with long linear test steps may execute OK, but they are hard to maintain. There is an important step missing: refactoring.

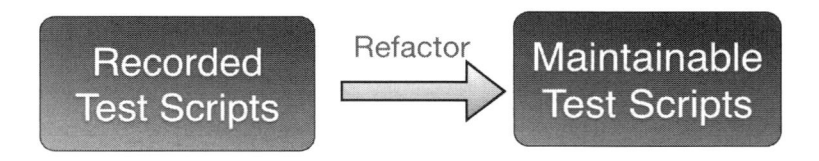

Recorded Test Scripts → Refactor → Maintainable Test Scripts

Functional test refactoring is a process of changing rudimentary test scripts into more maintainable test scripts. The rhythm of functional test refactoring is the same as code refactoring: "test, small change, test, small change". The meaning of 'test' (in the context functional test refactoring) is executing the automated tests.

Why do we need to do refactoring in small steps? As a human being, we make mistakes. By executing the test immediately after small changes, it will be easy to revert if the unexpected happens. When that happens, "Undo" is your best friend!

Tool Support

Refactoring is harder without good tool support, which makes code/test changes more reliable and much easier. If things are not easy to do, people just don't do them often. Now every major programming IDE supports various code refactorings.

There is a human factor too. During my programming career, I lost count of how many times I have written a coding standard (format of code) for the team. It always seemed that everyone's opinion was different, in the end nothing was changed. Once when all team members were required to use the same Java IDE which had a very nice code pretty printing feature, the previous individual opinions for coding layout suddenly disappeared.

Test scripts design and test practices can be highly subjective as well. Within a team, if tester A does not like the test scripts created by tester B, or vice versa, the test scripts are not going to be maintained easily. Good test tools can lead testers to reach a common understanding without losing flexibility.

Functional test refactoring is still a new concept. TestWise is one of a few test tools I know of (disclosure: I created TestWise) that supports some basic functional test refactorings. Next, we will improve a sample recorded test script to make it more maintainable by performing refactorings step by step.

Case Study

Test Case: In an online flight booking system (the one we used in Chapter 5), a user can sign in, select flight, enter passenger details and get a confirmation of their booking.

We have a test case with the recorder-generated test steps.

```
test_case "(Recorded version) Book Flight" do
  enter_text("username", "agileway")
  enter_text("password", "testwise")
  click_button("Sign in")
  click_radio_option("tripType", "return")
  select_option("fromPort", "New York")
  select_option("toPort", "Sydney")
  select_option("departDay", "03")
  select_option("departMonth", "September 2012")
  select_option("returnDay", "04")
  select_option("returnMonth", "October 2012")
  click_button("Continue")
  enter_text("passengerFirstName", "Bob")
  enter_text("passengerLastName", "The Tester")
  click_button("Next")

  click_radio_option("card_type", "master")
  enter_text("holder_name", "Bob the Tester")
  enter_text("card_number", "4242424242424242")
  select_option("expiry_month", "04")
  select_option("expiry_year", "2012")
  click_button("Pay now")
  try_for(15) { assert_text_present("Booking number")}

  expect(page_text).to include("New York to Sydney")
  expect(page_text).to include("Sydney to New York")
  assert_text_present("return Trip")
  assert_text_present("Bob The Tester")
  click_link("Sign off")
end
```

Extract "sign in" function

We identify the first 3 operations are performing a common sign-in operation, which will be heavily reused. Now we will extract them into a reusable function. Highlighting these 3 lines, go to the menu 'Refactor' → 'Extract to Function'

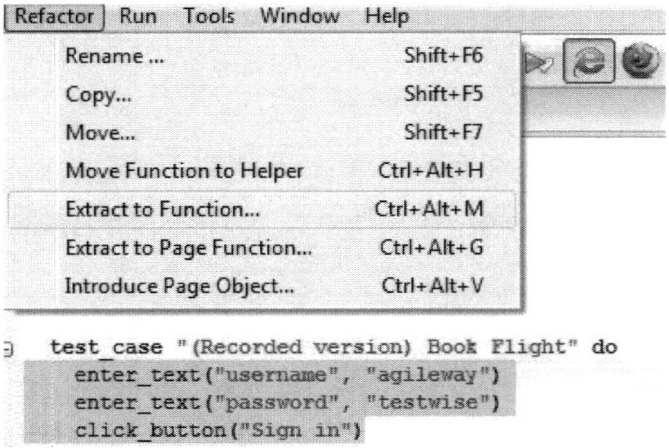
Refactor Run Tools Window Help
Rename ... Shift+F6
Copy... Shift+F5
Move... Shift+F7
Move Function to Helper Ctrl+Alt+H
Extract to Function... Ctrl+Alt+M
Extract to Page Function... Ctrl+Alt+G
Introduce Page Object... Ctrl+Alt+V
test_case "(Recorded version) Book Flight" do
enter_text("username", "agileway")
enter_text("password", "testwise")
click_button("Sign in")

Which will bring up a window to let you enter the function name and change parameters if needed

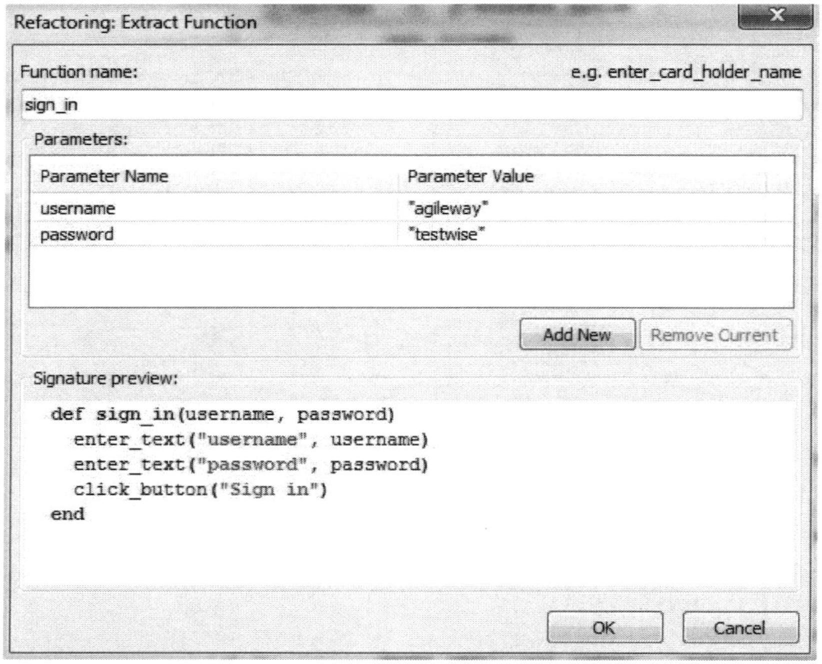
Refactoring: Extract Function
Function name:
e.g. enter_card_holder_name
sign_in
Parameters:
Parameter Name
Parameter Value
username
"agileway"
password
"testwise"
Add New
Remove Current
Signature preview:
def sign_in(username, password)
enter_text("username", username)
enter_text("password", password)
click_button("Sign in")
end
OK
Cancel

Press 'OK' button, the three test statements will be extracted in *sign_in* function and test scripts are updated accordingly.

```
14      def sign_in(username, password)
15        enter_text("username", username)
16        enter_text("password", password)
17        click_button("Sign in")
18      end
19
20      test_case "(Recorded version) Book Flight" do
21        sign_in("agileway", "testwise")
```

Rerun the test case.

Extract "sign off" function

The last statement (sign off) of our recorder-generated test steps.

```
click_link("Sign off")
```

is also a good candidate for a common function.

As there is only one line, just move the cursor to the line, press 'Ctrl' + 'Alt' + 'M' (keyboard shortcut to 'Extract to Function') to perform similar refactoring as above. We get the test script:

```
def sign_in(username, password)
  enter_text("username", username)
  enter_text("password", password)
  click_button("Sign in")
end

def sign_off
  click_link("Sign off")
end

test_case "(Recorded version) Book Flight" do
  sign_in("agileway", "testwise")

  # other test steps in between ...

  sign_off
end
```

Extract FlightPage

After a user logs in, they land on the flight page. We are going to introduce a FlightPage class here. First move the cursor to the first test operation on the flight page: select trip type, then navigate to menu 'Refactor' → 'Extract Page'

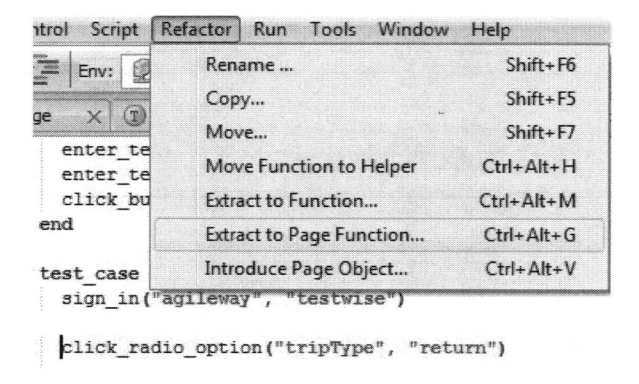

Enter page name: FlightPage and function name of the operation: *select_trip_type*

![Extract Page dialog showing Page Name: FlightPage, Function Name: select_trip_type, Parameter Name: trip_type, Parameter Value: "return". Preview: 'FlightPage' in file 'flight_page.rb']

```
def select_trip_type(trip_type)
    click_radio_option("tripType", trip_type)
end
```

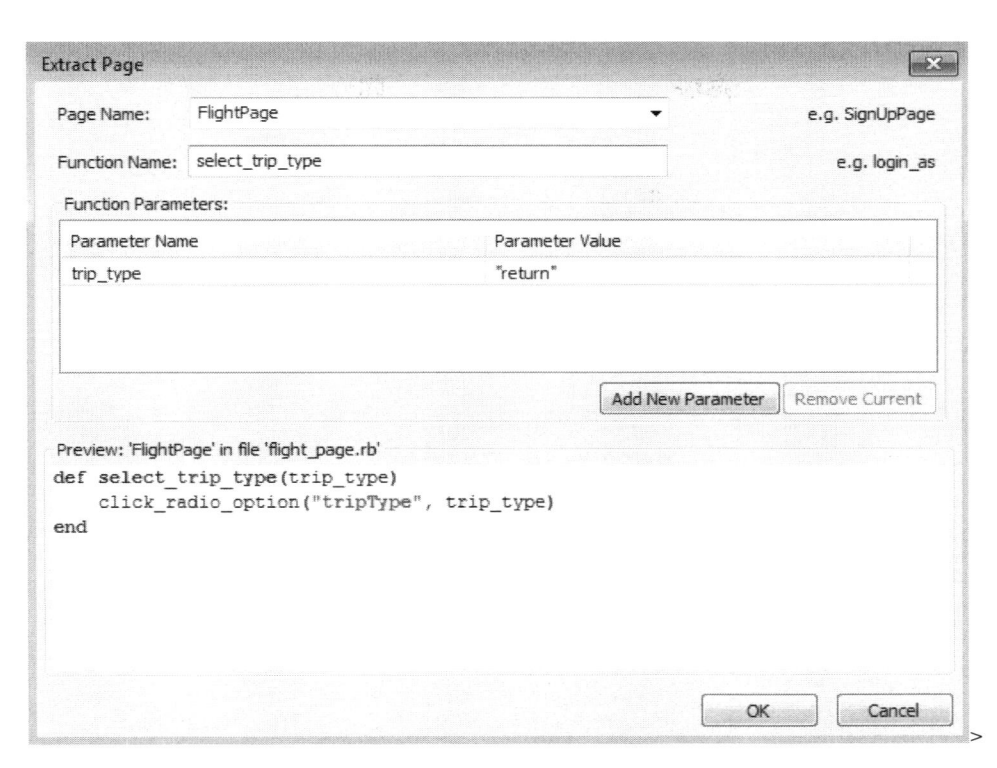

Press 'OK'. A new file *flight_page.rb* (under pages folder) will be created with *select_trip_type* function defined.

```
require File.join(File.dirname(__FILE__), "abstract_page.rb")

class FlightPage < AbstractPage
  def initialize(driver)
    super(driver, "") # <= TEXT UNIQUE TO THIS PAGE
  end

  def select_trip_type(trip_type)
    click_radio_option("tripType", trip_type)
  end

end
```

Next, the test case will be updated to use this newly created *FlightPage* class.

```
                test_case "(Refactored version) Book Flight" do
                  sign_in("agileway", "testwise")

                  flight_page = expect_page FlightPage
                  flight_page.select_trip_type("return")

                  select_option("fromPort", "New York")
```

Rerun the test and it should still pass. Then continue on the same Extract Page refactoring to the remaining test operations on the flight page.

```
#...
flight_page = expect_page FlightPage
flight_page.select_trip_type("return")
flight_page.select_from("New York")
flight_page.select_to("Sydney")
flight_page.select_departure_day("03")
flight_page.select_departure_month("September 2012")
flight_page.select_return_day("04")
flight_page.select_return_month("October 2012")
flight_page.click_continue
#...
```

Rerun the test.

Extract PassengerPage

Now we are on the passenger page to enter passenger details. We will introduce a new *PassengerPage* class. The process is the same as the previous step.

```
passenger_page = expect_page PassengerPage
passenger_page.enter_first_name("Bob")
passenger_page.select_last_name("The Tester")
passenger_page.click_next
```

Rerun the test.

Extract PaymentPage

Now we are reaching the final page: the payment page to pay with a credit card. Here we introduce a new *CreditCardPage* class.

```
credit_card_page = expect_page CreditCardPage
credit_card_page.enter_card_type("master")
credit_card_page.enter_holder_name("Bob the Tester")
credit_card_page.enter_card_number("4242424242424242")
credit_card_page.select_expiry_month("04")
credit_card_page.select_expiry_year("2012")
credit_card_page.click_pay_now
```

Rerun the test.

After clicking 'Pay now' button on the payment page, we will perform verification on the confirmation page. It is up to you whether or not to extract these assertions steps into a new ConfirmationPage class.

Move function to test helper

We want *sign_in* function to be available to all other test cases as well. To achieve this, we will move the function to the 'test helper' which is accessible to all test script files.

Move the cursor to the declaration of the *sign_in* function (between *sign_in* word as below), navigate to menu 'Refactor' → 'Move Function to Helper'.

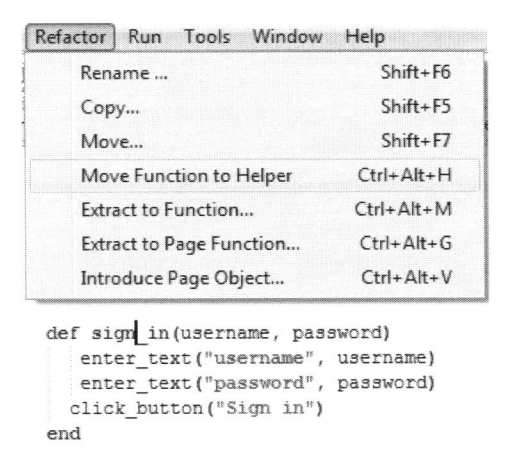

A confirmation popup window shows up, click OK.

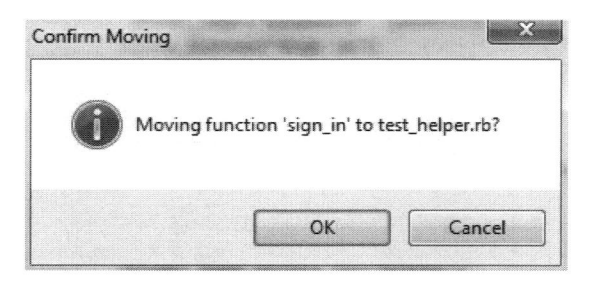

You will find the *sign_in* function is now moved to *test_helper.rb*.

Continue the Move Function to Helper refactoring (Ctrl + Alt + H) for *sign_off* function. After that, in *test_helper.rb*:

```
def sign_in(username, password)
    enter_text("username", username)
    enter_text("password", password)
    click_button("Sign in")
end
```

Rerun the test.

Move to execution hooks

Now our test case is a lot easier to read and maintain. While we are here, we can do one more refactoring. Let's say we are going to write a couple more test cases in this test script file. Before each test case, we sign in; after each test case, we sign out. We can utilize execution hooks in RSpec to further optimize the test script, that is, move sign in test steps to *before(:each)* and sign out test steps to *after(:each)*. A simple and effective way to achieve this is to use Move refactoring.

Move the cursor to the first line (*sign_in*), navigate to Menu 'Refactor' → 'Move'

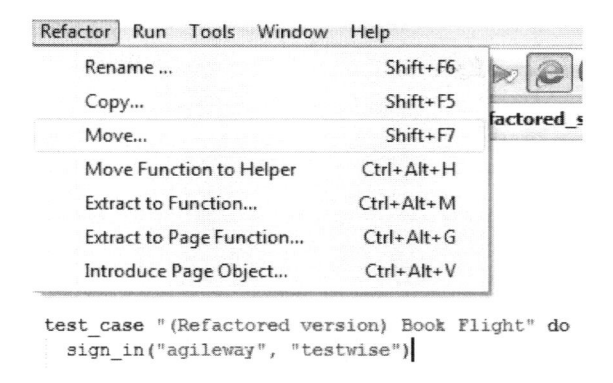

Select 'Move to before(:each)'

A confirmation popup window shows up to preview the refactoring change

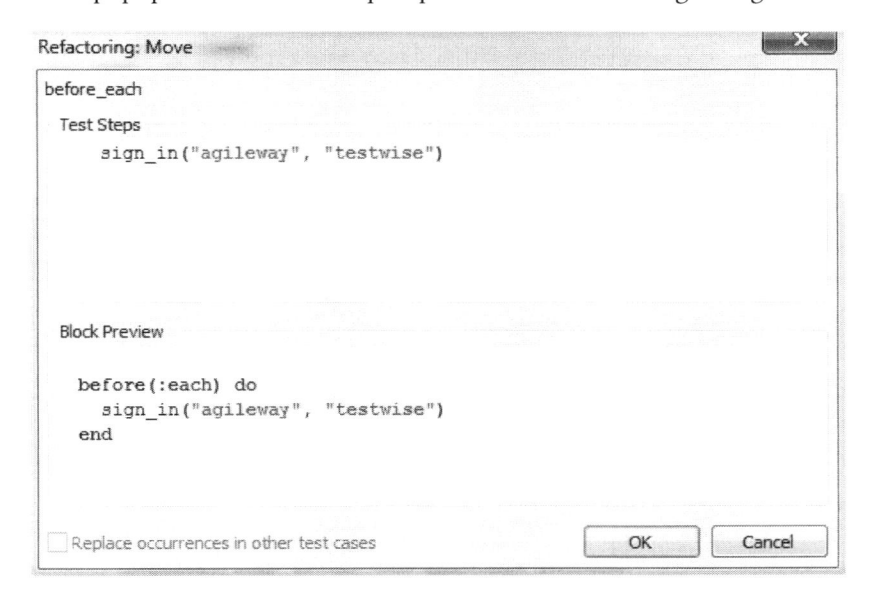

Click OK, the *sign_in(...)* call is moved from the test case to before(:each) block.

```
before(:each) do
  sign_in("agileway", "testwise")
end

test_case "(Refactored version) Book Flight" do
  flight_page = expect_page FlightPage
```

Perform another 'Move' refactoring to *sign_off* function, this time, select 'Move to after(:each)'.

Full test scripts

```
before(:each) do
  sign_in("agileway", "testwise")
end

after(:each) do
  sign_off unless debugging?
end

test_case "(Refactored version) Book Flight" do
  flight_page = expect_page FlightPage
  flight_page.select_trip_type("return")
  flight_page.select_from("New York")
  flight_page.select_to("Sydney")
  flight_page.select_departure_day("03")
  flight_page.select_departure_month("September 2012")
  flight_page.select_return_day("04")
  flight_page.select_return_month("October 2012")
  flight_page.click_continue

  passenger_page = expect_page PassengerPage
  passenger_page.enter_first_name("Bob")
  passenger_page.select_last_name("The Tester")
  passenger_page.click_next

  credit_card_page = expect_page CreditCardPage
  credit_card_page.select_card_type("master")
  credit_card_page.enter_holder_name("Bob the Tester")
  credit_card_page.enter_card_number("4242424242424242")
```

```
  credit_card_page.select_expiry_month("04")
  credit_card_page.select_expiry_year("2012")
  credit_card_page.click_pay_now

  try_for(15) { assert_text_present("Booking number")}
  expect(page_text).to include("New York to Sydney")
  expect(page_text).to include("Sydney to New York")
  assert_text_present("return Trip")
  assert_text_present("Bob The Tester")
end
```

Summary

In Chapter 5, we created 6 test cases (in four test scripts files) for the same sample site. In this chapter, we applied some refactorings to recorder-generated test scripts, namely:

- Extract function (sign_in, *sign_off*)
- Move (*sign_in* and *sign_off*) to Helper
- Extract page class (*FlightPage*, *PassengerPage*, *CreditCardPaymentPage*)
- Move (to execution hooks)

One thing we haven't covered is the reuse of existing page classes in new tests. For this test case in *passenger_spec.rb*,

```
test_case "Can enter passenger details (watir)" do
  browser.radio(:name => "tripType", :value => "return").click
  ...
end
```

The first test step is an operation on the flight page and we already have *FlightPage* extracted (if you refactored *flight_spec.rb* first). Obviously we want to use the *FlightPage* class. Here is how:

1. Type 'ep' (for *expect_page*) then press Tab key to show defined page classes (in a list), and select 'FlightPage'

```
browser.radio(:name => "tripType", :value => "return").click
expect_page |
            ┌─────────────────────────────────┐
            │ (p) AbstractPage                │
            │ (p) FlightPage                  │
            └─────────────────────────────────┘
```

1. Select menu 'Refactor' → 'Introduce page object...'

```
browser.radio(:name => "tripType", :value => "return").click
flight_page = expect_page FlightPage
```

1. Type 'flight_page.' and select operation 'select_trip_type'

```
browser.radio(:name => "tripType", :value => "return").click
flight_page = expect_page FlightPage
flight_page.select_t|
browser.sel ┌──────────────────────────────────┐
browser.sel │ (f) select_trip_type             │
            └──────────────────────────────────┘
```

1. Delete the recorded test step (as now it has been replaced with a call to a page operation)

```
browser.radio(:name => "tripType", :value => "return").click
flight_page = expect_page FlightPage
flight_page.select_trip_type("return")
```

You can find all six refactored test cases under *sources\ch08-refactoring\refactor_case_study*. If you use TestWise, try to invoke refactorings by using keyboard shortcuts, you will be surprised how much faster you'll be at writing the test script and how quickly you will memorize the shortcut keys.

9. Review

Some readers might have already started writing tests for their work. That's great! You now have all the knowledge you need for developing maintainable automated tests. However, there is another obstacle to overcome, although it won't be obvious until you have developed a fair amount of tests.

In this chapter, I will cover some common challenges or questions you might face now.

Syntax Errors

Test scripts are written in a certain syntax (all test scripts covered in this book are in Ruby). Test scripts simply won't run if there are syntax errors in them. And syntax errors can be frustrating, particularly for beginners.

Let's see some examples.

```ruby
describe "Test Suite" do
  # ...

  it "A Test" do
    enter_text("username", "VALUE")
  end
end

end
```

The above test fails to execute due to invalid test script syntax: an extra *end*. In Ruby, *do ... end* (another form: *{ ... }*) mark the scope of test steps. To fix the above the test scripts: just simply delete one *'end'* (which one doesn't really matter in the case above).

Another common error is non matching quotes or parentheses, like the one below:

```
test_case "no matching quotes" do
  enter_text("surname", 'O'sullivan')
end
```

The single or double quotes are used to mark strings. If the string contains quotes, they need to be escaped like below:

```
enter_text("surname", 'O\'sullivan') # escaping single quote ' using \
enter_text("surname", "O'sullivan") # or using different quote delimiter ""
```

How to avoid?

- **Syntax validator**

    Invoking a syntax validator is the most effective way to identify syntax errors, and it is easy when test scripts are being developed in testing IDEs. The below is the validation output for our first sample test script in TestWise.

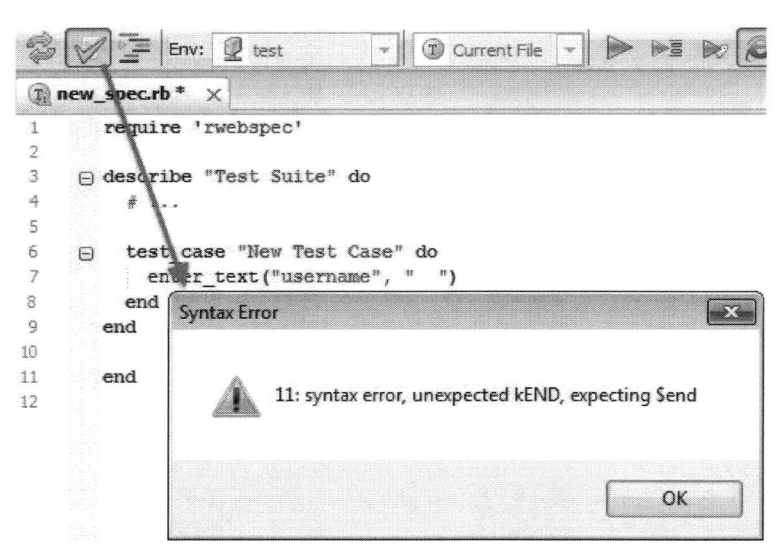

    TestWise Validator

- **Use editor/IDE with syntax highlighting**

    In editors/IDEs that support Ruby syntax highlighting, it can become clear where syntax errors are:

```
22      test_case "no matching quotes" do
23        enter_text("surname", 'O''sullivan')
24      end
```
Syntax highlighting in TestWise

- **Indenting tests scripts well**

  Mis-indented test scripts can cause visual confusion, and make it hard to identify syntax errors.

- **Use Undo**

  Reverting recent changes back to a working state. This rather simple approach can actually be quite effective.

Having worked with quite a few programming and test script languages, personally I found Ruby syntax is the most intuitive one.

Set up source control

It surprises me that so many projects are not using source control systems (SCS) to version control their test scripts, they version control the program code, why not the test scripts? With test scripts in SCS, changes are tracked (and can be reversed when necessary) and team collaboration is possible. Don't worry that you don't have working experience with source control, it is actually quite easy. Next I will show you how to set up one for your own use and possible sharing with your colleagues.

There are many commercial and free source control systems, my recommendation is Git. Since there are many Git tutorial and online resources available, I will keep my instructions focusing on the needs for testing.

Git Installation

Here I will cover Git on Windows (Git is included in some Linux distributions and on Mac after installing XCode). Thanks to the installer (http://git-scm.com/download/win), the installation is quick and easy. After the installation, for convenience, add your git bin path (e.g. `c:\apps\Git-1.9.5-preview20141217\bin`) to your PATH environment variables.

Set up Git for local working folder

Assume you have a working folder: c:\work\project_abc\test_scripts.

Start Windows command window (press Win+R, enter 'cmd' and press Enter). Here I will show you how to execute commands by typing them rather than using some kind of GUI tool. Some might not be used to this, but I strongly recommend you to try it. It is not hard. More importantly, executing a large number of tests is always better done from the command line.

Set up git repository for this folder (this will create a hidden folder named '.git').

```
> cd c:\work\project_abc\test_scripts
> git init
```

To add all existing files (recursively) in the folder to Git.

```
> git add .
```

To commit (also known as check-in).

```
> git commit -a -m "description of changes"
```

To check recent log entries.

```
> git log
```

To discard changes you have made, ie, revert to the last revision in Git. You may specify which revision on which file by providing more parameters.

```
> git checkout -f
```

Set up Git for a shared folder on NetWork Drive

Usually it is a good idea to set up a 'parent' Git repository. Besides the assurance of a back up, more importantly, you will be able to collaborate among the team members (we will cover more on this in the next chapter). An ideal location for a parent repository is on the network drive.

Create a new folder on a network drive (let's assume G:\ is a network drive).

```
> cd G:\teams\project_abc\testing
> mkdir test_scripts
> cd test_scripts
```

Set up Git. By specifying flag `--bare`, there will be no working files.

```
> git init --bare
```

Change to our working folder and 'assign' a 'parent' to our local git repository.

```
> cd c:\work\project_abc\test_scripts
> git remote add origin  G:\teams\project_abc\testing\test_scripts
```

And push local changes to the parent repository

```
> git push origin master
```

Frequently used Git commands after set up

To get new changes from the 'parent repository' (your colleagues might have checked-in new tests)

```
> cd c:\work\project_abc\test_scripts
> git pull
```

To commit your changes and make them available to other team members.

```
> git commit -a -m "local new changes"
> git push
```

GUI/Object Map

GUI map or object map is a file containing variables to controls in GUI applications, a fairly common approach used in some commercial or home-grown testing test tools. The purpose of a GUI map is to enhance maintainability of test scripts, similar to Page object pattern.

One's understanding of GUI map can be quite different from another's, and I haven't seen one working test automation solution with an implementation of GUI maps. If you are comfortable with reusable functions and page objects (covered in early chapters), you can simply ignore object map (or similar) concepts.

Page objects is a well established pattern for automated testing (Selenium Wiki has a good page on it: http://code.google.com/p/selenium/wiki/PageObjects). In later chapters, you will see how easy and powerful page objects can be adapted to other test frameworks.

Custom Libraries

Some technical testers (especially with programming skills) often rush to develop modularized libraries. For example, the test scripts below use the functions defined in two modules *login.rb* and *payment.rb*:

```ruby
require 'c:/testprojects/foo/login.rb'
require 'c:/testprojects/foo/payment.rb'

describe "Payment with Credit Card" do
  include Login
  include Payment

  it "Test case 1" do
    # use functions defined in login.rb
    # ...
    # use functions defined in payment.rb
  end
end
```

I cannot say that the approach is wrong, but I am concerned with the complexity and the lack of convention in the test scripts. For some big test automation solutions I was involved with, that had a large number of automated tests running for hours, the test project structure was not much different from what you saw in Chapter 8. That is, only one *test_helper.rb* plus many page classes.

I am not discouraging testers to use their creativity here, instead I suggest testers, especially those who are new to test automation and Ruby, focusing on writing quality tests with known working convention first. Let's examine the first two lines of the above test scripts:

```
require 'c:/testprojects/foo/login.rb'
require 'c:/testprojects/foo/payment.rb'
```

There are two issues. It is clear that the test folder is `c:\testprojects\foo`, however, what happens if your test project folder changes? The tests will fail. Also in Ruby, `require` means it only needs to be loaded once, that is, updates to *login.rb* or *payment.rb* wouldn't take effect unless you restart your IDE.

Debugging

Debugging is a term mostly used by programmers. It means to analyze and remove bugs in the code. In the context of automated functional testing for websites, debugging is to find out why a test step did not execute as expected. For example, test execution stopped because it was unable to locate a button to click or failed an assertion of the text on a web page. The causes usually fit in one of the categories below:

- real application error detected
- the web page changed (unexpected or expected but the test scripts not updated yet)
- error exists in test scripts (hey testers make errors too!)

The context determines the debugging approach and tools for functional test scripts are different from the ones used by programmers. Testers with strong programming background should especially pay attention. During code debugging, the complex nature of software requires sophisticated debugging capability such as object inspection, watch, step in, step out, and so on. In test script debugging, it is a lot simpler.

If test execution failed on a test step, a tester's immediate reaction is to analyze the content of the current page (stopping at the failing point) against the test step. There is no difference between manual and automated testing here. To be able to inspect, we want to stop at the web page where the failure occurred and remain in the browser. In TestWise, when you run an individual (as opposed to the suite) test case, the browser will be left open after the execution is complete. However, we cannot do that for running multiple tests in one go.

Typically, when automation testers work against a new software build or conduct tests against a target module, they should work like this:

1. Run a group of automated tests (which may be across multiple files)
2. Identify failed ones from the test report (or console output)
3. Run individual test (start debugging)
4. Analyze test script, application (web page in browser) and requirement to identify the cause
5. Update the test scripts and rerun (go to step 3) as necessary
6. Move on to the next failed test (go to step 3) until all resolved

There are more advanced debugging techniques, which maybe tools dependent. TestWise professional edition provides more debugging features such as run to certain test step and run selected test steps against current browser.

10. Collaboration

> "*Teamwork* : n. Cooperative effort by the members of a group or team to achieve a common goal." - American Heritage Dictionary of the English Language, Fourth Edition

Coding and testing are usually the two most important activities in a software project. For a successful software project, it is essential to have efficient and healthy collaboration (i.e. teamwork) between programmers and testers.

In this chapter, we will see how collaboration works with automated functional testing through UI with three scenarios.

Pre-requisite

Version Control Server

A version control (also known as source control) server is a central repository for a project's source code, tests and other important files. Apart from keeping project artifacts safe (if backed up properly), a version control system keeps the history of changes. Git and Subversion are the two most popular open-source VCS.

A typical use of version control server in a software team is like this:

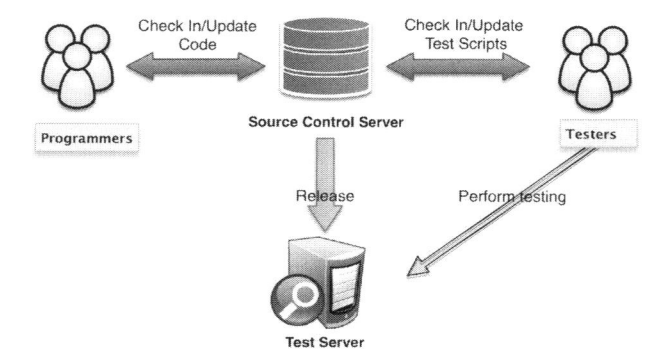

Programmers use VCS to work collaboratively on coding among themselves. We could use existing infrastructure in place to support collaboration between programmers and testers as well.

Same Testing Tool

Testers and programmers access the test scripts (and others) from the same version control server. To minimise unnecessary confusion, both of them should use the same testing tool.

I will use TestWise for case studies in this chapter. For non-TestWise users, it is quite easy to achieve the function required for team collaboration:

- Changing target server to run tests against. Simply modify the site URL constant in *test_helper.rb*

In the scenarios below, I will introduce two personas: Tom the tester and Paul the programmer.

Scenario 1: "It worked on my machine"

"*It worked on my machine*" is one of the most popular excuses used by programmers. It is not hard to understand why some programmers can get defensive on receiving defect reports. A programmer's profession is to produce working code. Imagine you are a programmer, a tester comes to your cubicle and tells you that your work is defected in front of other fellow programmers, as below:

Tom comes to Paul's desk with a defect report.

Tom: "Excuse me, Paul. User story 123: Admin user can login failed on this morning's build."
Paul: "Really" (*examining the report...*)
Tom: "I double checked, just then."
Paul: "It worked on my machine, I can show you."

(*Paul demonstrating on his development server..*)

Paul: "See, it is working. Are you sure you typed the password properly?"
Tom: "Yes, Why don't you try it on the test server?"
Paul: "All right." (*unwillingly*)

(*Paul tries it on the test server...*)

Paul: "Hmmm ..., It did fail, oh well, I will get back to you."

To make collaboration work, we need to reduce this kind of confrontation. Automated testing can help on this. Let's see that scenario again:

Tom: "Paul, user story 123 Admin user can login failed on this morning's build."
Paul: "Thanks, I will check in a few minutes."

(*Later..., Paul starts to investigate this defect*)

1. Perform source update (from VCS) to get latest test scripts
2. Open test tool TestWise, navigate to the test case for story 123

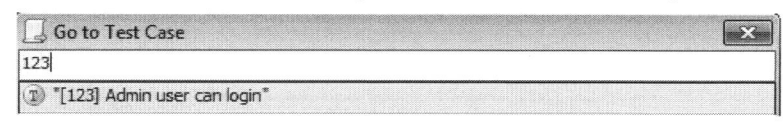

3. Run the test locally first, it is OK

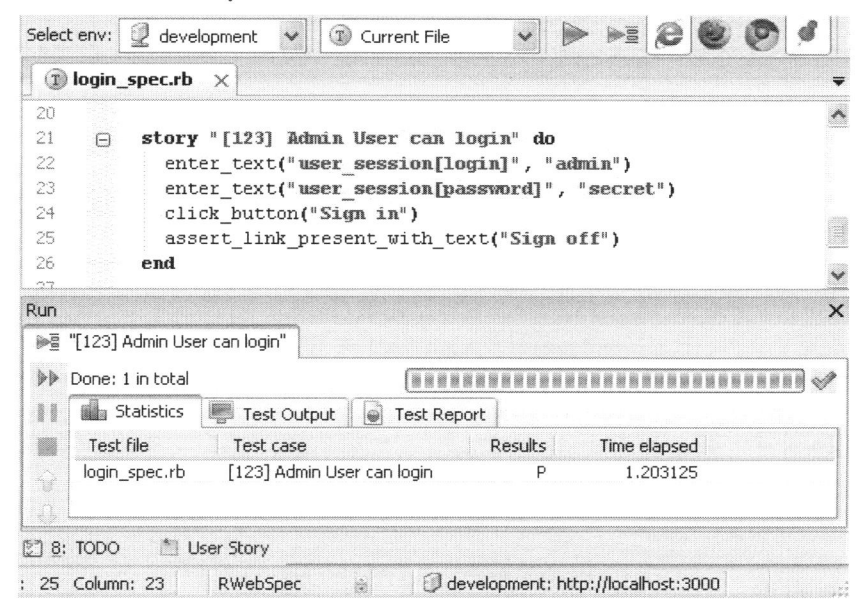

4. Change the target environment to the **test server**

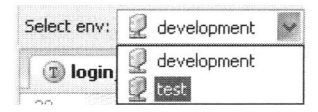

5. The same test failed on the **test server**

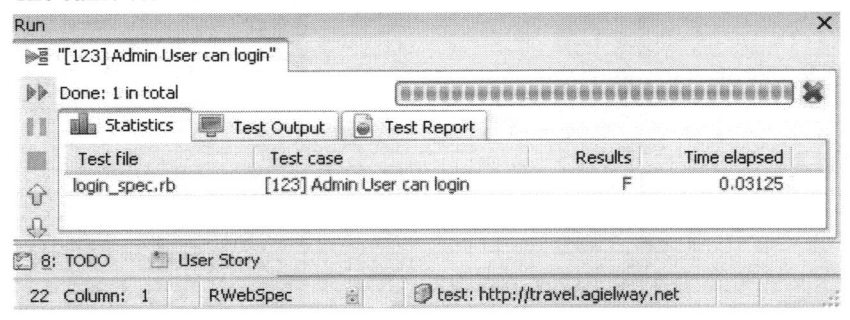

```
Run                                                                    X
  ▶ "[123] Admin User can login"
  ▶▶ Done: 1 in total            [████████████████████████████]  ✖
  ‖    Statistics   Test Output   Test Report
       Test file         Test case                    Results   Time elapsed
       login_spec.rb     [123] Admin User can login      F         0.03125

  8: TODO       User Story
  22  Column: 1      RWebSpec           test: http://travel.agielway.net
```

Paul: "Tom, I found the problem, and replicated the error on my local environment. It will be fixed in next build."

(*After a new build deployed*)

Tom: "Paul, just let you know, issue with user story 123 is now fixed, thanks."

Benefits

Avoid misunderstandings

As both programmers and testers run the same test script, and can see the execution in a browser, there is little room for misunderstandings.

No disruption

Testers can report the defect and continue performing other testing. Programmers can calmly finish their work at hand before addressing the defect.

No confrontation

No embarrassment for both programmers and testers (testers can make mistakes for raising false alarms as well).

Scenario 2: Synergy

Testers' lack of skills in programming and HTML knowledge is one of the most common reasons why projects don't do well in web test automation (when there are no technical testers or hands-on test coaches on board). Ironically, programmers in the team have the skills and share the same goal as testers, why don't the testers just ask them for help?

Some might say "we testers need to perform independent checks on programmers' work", which sounds about right. But frankly, I have never experienced 'compromise of independence' when testers and programmers were working closely. For start, testers design the test case and only seek help from programmers on specific technical difficulties. Furthermore, as test execution can be seen in browser, testers are verifying their independently designed test case.

The scenario 2 shows that Tom the tester encountered one hurdle on developing an automated test script and received help from a programmer.

Tom was running an automated test suite against the new build. He found that one previously working test created yesterday now failed. There were no signs of changes on the page where failure occurred.

Here is the test case

```
test_case "[123] Can create a new loan application" do
  new_loan_application_page = expect_page NewLoanApplicationPage
  new_loan_application_page.enter_app_number("L0123456")
  #...
end
```

and the page class (in *new_loan_application_page.rb*)

```
class NewLoanApplicationPage
    ...
  def enter_app_number(app_no)
    text_field(:id, "ctl00_dcb0d043_e7f0_4128_99c6_71c113f45dd8_AppName").se\
t app_no
  end
    ...
end
```

The error was "*Unable to locate element, using :id, 'ctl00_dcb0d043_e7f0_4128_99c6_71c113f45dd8_-AppName'*" and the error trace pointed to the failing line was at entering text in application number text box. Paul remembered he created this test step with a recorder, and it worked then.

The HTML fragment source was

```
<input id="ct100_dcb0d043_e7f0_4128_99c6_71c113f45dd8_AppName" type="text"
name="ct100$m$g_dcb0d043_e7f0_4128_99c6_71c113f45dd8$ct100$tAppName"/>
```

Now in the new build, it was changed to:

```
<input id="ct100_dcb9d014_g7f0_7188_98c6_71d123f45ed7_AppName" type="text"
name="ct100$m$g_dcb9d014_g7f0_7188_98c6_71d123f45ed7$ct100$tAppName"/>
```

In HTML source, the 'id' and 'name' of the text box were changed. Frustrated, Tom contacted Paul the programmer for help.

Tom: "Paul, the HTML ID of application number text box on entering new loan application page has been changed in the new build."
Paul: "Yes, the page is dynamically generated from a framework. A long unique identifier is prefixed by the system, not us."
Tom: "But this makes our testing very difficult. Can you help?"
Paul: "OK, send me some information and see what I can do."
Tom: "Thanks in advance." *(sending the following in email)*

> Paul,
>
> You start TestWise, open the test project (c:\work\ui-tests\ui-tests.tpr) if not already opened.
>
> The failure occurs at *new_loan_application_page.rb*. You can navigate to it quickly this way: 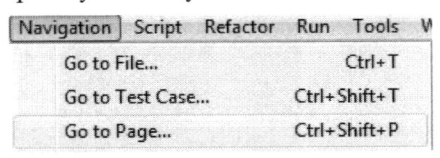
>
> | Navigation | Script | Refactor | Run | Tools |
> |---|---|---|---|---|
> | Go to File... | | | Ctrl+T | |
> | Go to Test Case... | | | Ctrl+Shift+T | |
> | Go to Page... | | | Ctrl+Shift+P | |
>
> Type in 'newloan' will narrow down to the page, press 'Enter'. 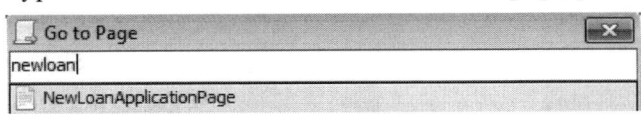
>
> Go to Page
> newloan
> NewLoanApplicationPage
>
> To run the test case,
>
> | Navigation | Version Control | Script | Refactor |
> |---|---|---|---|
> | Go to File... | | Ctrl+T | |
> | Go to Test Case... | | Ctrl+Shift+T | |

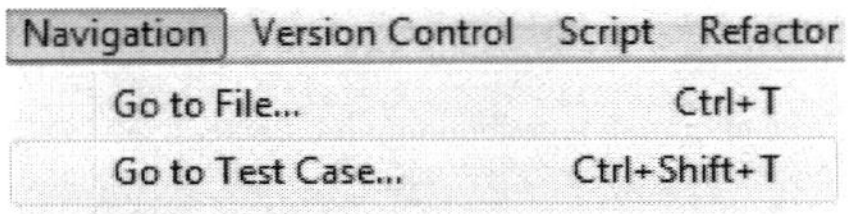

In the dialog, type in 'loan' will narrow down to the test case quickly. Then press 'Enter'

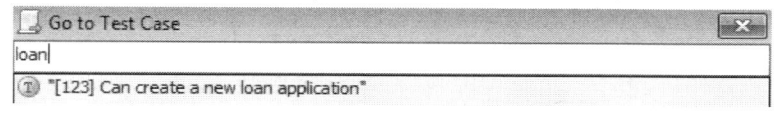

```
Go to Test Case
loan
[123] Can create a new loan application
```

Right click in any line between the test case, select first run menu

```
test_case "[123] Can create a new loan application" do
  new_loan_application_page = expect_page NewLoanApplicationPage
  new_loan_application_page.enter_app_number("L0123456")
  # ...
end        Run _case "[123] Can create a new loan a..."   Ctrl+Shift+F10
```

Thanks,
Tom

Paul: "Got your email. I ran the test and can see where it's failing. Though the prefix part may change between builds, the ending part, as I set it, does not change. We can probably try to use regular expression to identify the element. I am not familiar to Watir. Let me google some examples."

(*several minutes later*)

Paul: "Tom, I got it working. I checked the updated page class into the source control."

(*Tom performed update from source control server and got updated page class.*)

```
class NewLoanApplicationPage
    ...
  def enter_app_number(app_no)
    text_field(:id, /AppName$/).set app_no
  end
    ...
end
```

(*Ran the test, it now passed*)

Tom: "Thanks a lot! You saved my day."

Benefits

The benefit is obvious, without programmers' help, some automated tests might not be done. This type of communication helps programmers to be more aware of testers' work as well. Thus they are more likely to take this into consideration for software development, i.e, more test friendly design. The payoff for that is huge.

Scenario 3: Acceptance Test Driven Development

Test Driven Development (TDD) is an important practice of agile methodologies which turns tradition development process around: programmers write unit tests before code. Studies show TDD make programmers more productive.

ATDD is a variation of TDD. In ATDD, simply speaking, testers write automated tests as executable requirements first with the help of customers, then programmers implement software features to pass these tests. When all tests have passed, the development is complete. A large percentage of acceptance tests in ATDD are functional tests via the user interface.

You may ask: How could we write tests before it is implemented? Let's look at this scenario.

Tom the tester is assigned to work on the test case for requirement: User can change password. This feature is not implemented yet. But Tom has the wireframe from business analysts, and he understands this requirement well.

Change Password

Current Password	
New Password	
Password Confirmation	

[Change]

He opens the testing tool (TestWise) and writes (and verifies) test steps to get the browser to the screen where the 'Change Password' link will be added.

```
before(:all) do
  open_browser
  sign_in("bob")
end

before(:each) do
  click_link("User Profile")
end

test_case "User can change password" do
  # add test steps here
end
```

Tom starts to write the first test step for the operation that does not exist: click 'Change Password' link.

```
test_case "User can change password" do
  click_link("Change Password")
end
```

According to the wireframe, this will be a new page that allows users to enter the new password. Tom types in next test statement:

```
expect_page ChangePasswordPage
```

move the cursor in 'ChangePasswordPage' text, press 'Alt + Space'

```
story "User can change password" do
  click_link("Change Password")
  expect_page ChangePasswordPage
```
    Create page class 'ChangePasswordPage'
en
    Press Up, Down and Enter to select, Press Esc to close dialog

Press 'Enter' to create the new page class *ChangePasswordPage* in file *change_password_page.rb*

```
Project: ch08.tpr                           password_spec.rb    ×    change_password_page.rb *  ×
  ch10-collaboration                     1      require File.join(File.dirname(__FILE__), "abstract_page.rb")
    pages                                2
      abstract_page.rb                   3      class ChangePasswordPage < AbstractPage
      change_password_page.rb            4
    spec                                 5        def initialize(driver)
      login_spec.rb                      6          super(driver, "Page Text") # <= TEXT UNIQUE TO THIS PAGE
      password_spec.rb                   7        end
```

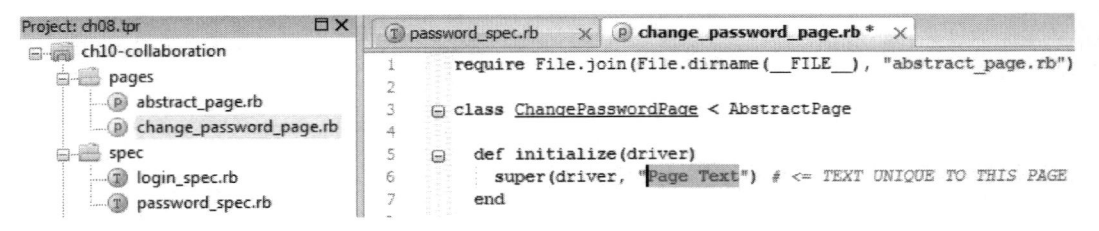

Tom enters the heading text on the page 'Change Password', then goes back to the test case. Tom enters first test step on the change password page: enter the current password,

```
change_password_page.enter_current_password("test")
```

Move the cursor under 'enter_current_password'. Press 'Alt + Space', which shows suggested actions for the test statement.

```
change_password_page = expect_page ChangePasswordPage
change_password_page.enter_current_password("test")
    Create function 'enter_current_password' in page class 'ChangePasswordPage'
```

Press 'Enter'. A new empty function will be created in *ChangePasswordPage*,

```
class ChangePasswordPage < AbstractPage

  def initialize(driver)
    super(driver, "Change Password") # <= TEXT UNIQUE
  end

  def enter_current_password(current_password="test")
    # to be implemented
  end
```

Continue in the same way for remaining test steps on the change password page. Once all are completed, the full test script might look like this:

```
test_case "User can change password" do
  click_link("Change Password")
  change_password_page = expect_page ChangePasswordPage
  change_password_page.enter_current_password("test")
  change_password_page.enter_new_password("newone")
  change_password_page.enter_password_confirmation("newone")
  change_password_page.click_change

  sign_out
  sign_in("bob", "newone")
  assert_text_present("Welcome Bob")
end
```

From Tom's point of view, the test case is complete. However, it will fail on execution, as the feature is not implemented yet. Tom then add two files (one for test case and one for page class) into the source control.

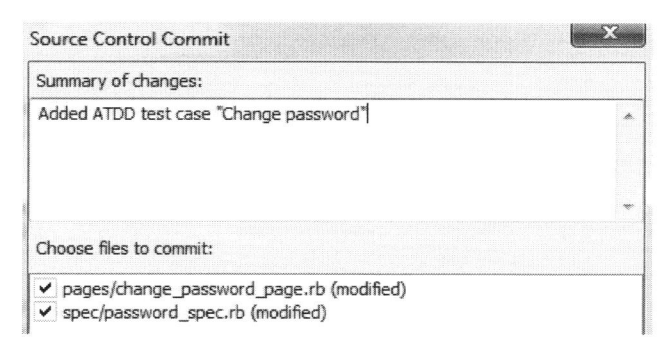

Paul the programmer is assigned to work on the feature. He performs source update and finds the test case and the incompleted *ChangePasswordPage* class.

```ruby
class ChangePasswordPage < AbstractPage

  def initialize(driver)
    super(driver, "Change Password")
  end

  def enter_current_password(current_password="test")
    # to be implemented
  end

  def enter_new_password(new_password="newone")
    # to be implemented
  end

  def enter_password_confirmation(password_confirmation="newone")
    # to be implemented
  end

  def click_change
    # to be implemented
  end

end
```

Paul starts to develop this feature, using the test case as a guideline. During the development, he might fill in the missing test steps in *ChangePasswordPage* or get the tester to do it.

```ruby
def enter_current_password(current_password="test")
  enter_text("current_pass", current_password)
end
```

Along the way, Paul runs the test case for self-verification until his implementation passes the test.

Benefits

Feeling of Achievement

Besides other ATDD pros and cons you may find in textbooks or the Internet, here I just want to point out one: "*It feels good!*" (if done properly). For testers, the 'table' has now turned around (we now guide programmers). The feeling of being in control is good. For programmers, with the target test in hand, the uncertainty of requirement changes is reduced and the sense of achievement is great when seeing a green tick (pass) on the test.

Wrap up

Effective tester-programmer collaboration needs a good foundation:

- Simple and easy to understand test framework
- Test script repository
- Easy to use testing tool

11. Continuous Integration with Functional Tests

> "Continuous Integration doesn't get rid of bugs, but it does make them dramatically easier to find and remove." – Martin Fowler

Still remember the Test Automation Camel metaphor in Chapter 1? We covered the first hump 'Hard to maintain' in Chapter 7 and 8. In this chapter we will look at the second major challenge of test automation: long feedback loop.

Long feedback loop

> "Automated tests don't have much value if they aren't giving you feedback several times a day." - Lisa Crispin [Crispin 08]

Once I had a conversation with a university professor at a testing conference. She told me that her students (majoring in software engineering) were required to write automated tests for a programming assignment. I said *"Let me guess, the starting part was easy, then they found it very hard after developed dozens of tests?"* She answered *"Yes."*

This happens to real software projects as well. Some find the effort to maintain automated tests seems to grow exponentially. If you have addressed the first hump ('Hard to maintain') properly (with good test script design and capable testing tools), updating test scripts with identified application changes should be easy. However, the next challenge will gradually start to emerge: after total execution time exceeds 1 hour (or less), it will become apparent. This challenge is 'long feedback loop', the second hump. It is the long time gap between the time when a programmer made one application change and when (automated) test failures (caused by the change) are detected.

As the time taken for deployment and execution of (all) test cases is long, both programmers and testers are likely move on to other tasks. By the time the test results (with failures) come out, programmers might have forgotten about the changes which might have caused it. While programmers are still trying to identify and fix the errors from previous test report, there might be some new defects found in another test execution. Experienced agile managers will stop all development on new features, and ask the team to focus on fixing defects. You can see, this kind of situation is not ideal.

There are human factors too. Human beings usually don't mind related interruptions during (or immediately after) their activities. But if programmers and testers just got their brains focused on new tasks, interruptions are not well received. Subconsciously, testers tend to not run regression tests as often, which makes the time gap even bigger. This can eventually lead to test automation failures.

The root of the problem is that functional testing via GUI is slow (comparing to programmer tests), and there is not much that testers can do to speed up the test execution of an individual automated test via GUI. But we can improve the feedback time when executing multiple (especially a large number of) automated tests, that is where Continuous Integration can help.

Prioritizing Tests is a bad idea

While working with testers, I found 'prioritizing tests' is a common (and instinctive) approach to deal with a large number of test cases. In my opinion, this approach might be effective for manual testing, but it certainly is not suitable to test automation.

As we know, the inevitable outcome of prioritizing tests is that tests with lower priority don't get run often. Now I want to ask, given maintaining the automated tests to keep up with application changes is a known challenge, what is the chance of being able to maintain those labelled as non-important (which don't get run often)? You might as well delete them rather than pretend you can maintain them. Remember, outdated tests cause confusion.

Personally, I don't remember needs (or efforts) for prioritizing tests in projects that implemented test automation well. We always tried making all tests correct and pass, and running all automated tests at least once a day. For the tests that are unstable or very difficult to conduct, we simply removed it from automated test suite, added it to manual test suite and acknowledged the risk.

Some may start to wonder is it possible to run all tests everyday? A simple answer is to distribute tests to multiple machines and execute them in parallel. Nowadays, computers are relatively cheap (when compared with the cost of labour). The cost of one or more test prioritization meetings might be enough to buy several test machines.

Continuous Integration

Continuous Integration (CI) is "a software development practice where members of a team integrate their work frequently" [Fowler 00]. The aim of CI is to produce builds and passing automated tests many times a day.

Ever since Martin Fowler published his famous "Continuous Integration" article, CI has become a hot topic in software development world. However, as Martin pointed out, "Software development is full of best practices which are often talked about but seem to be rarely done" [Fowler 00]. CI is one of them. I remember at a software conference, one delegate talked about why he attended the conference: "I want to know how other projects are doing CI? The closest to CI I ever encountered was one machine was assigned to be the CI server, then ticked the box. No one touched the machine again."

Continuous Integration and Testing

> "If I had to pick one reason our team has been so successful the past 7 years, our CI process is it" – Lisa Crispin

For readers who still have doubts on the value of CI in testing, I can tell you, the two topics (CI and testing) are closely related. In fact there is a world-wide conference just named Continuous Integration and Testing Conference (CITCON).

CI Build Steps

Continuous Integration, simply put, is to run a server to check the source control for new changes and then run a series of build tasks (testings are build tasks in CI). Some common build tasks are listed below in the order of execution:

- Source and test scripts checkout from the VCS
- Database migration
- Code compilation
- Unit testing
- Code coverage
- Package
- Deployment

- Functional UI testing
- Tagging the release in VCS
- Notification

Here is a diagram

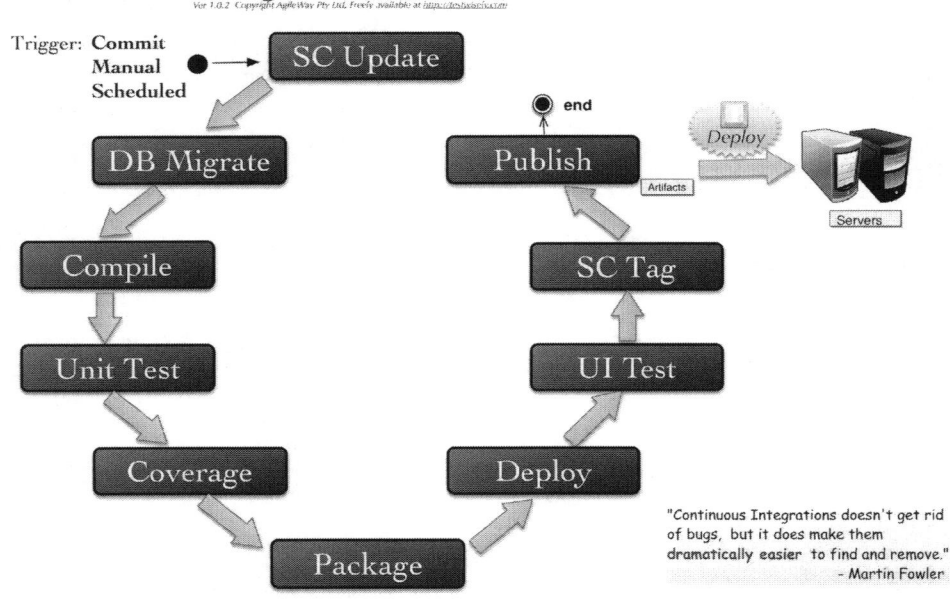

CI in nutshell

A failure in one build step will exit the whole build process. In other words, a good build must pass all the specified build steps.

Our focus in this book is the functional UI testing step, an important but often neglected step. Why is it important? Only comprehensive functional UI testing can provide assurance that the build that actually meets the requirements. Without it, the whole process is not fully automated, and the team will lack confidence to deploy generated build to a ready-to-demo environment straight way.

The functional UI testing step, in my opinion, is also the most challenging one. For start, a solid maintainable test automation solution needs to be in place, which few projects have achieved that (not for your project though, as you are going to implement it after reading this book, right?). Executing functional tests frequently requires a highly reliable execution environment, as UI test execution is vulnerable to external environmental events, such as: OS restart after auto updates, system slow down due to the start of anti-virus checking, ..., etc.

Functional UI Test Build Step with Rake

Executing a build step means to invoke a pre-defined build task in a build language, such as Ant in Java, MSBuild in .NET and Rake in Ruby. So far, we have been running automated tests in Testing IDEs (such as TestWise) or from the command line (as shown in Chapter 2). To manage frequent and a large volume of test execution of automated tests, we need to use build scripts which provide more flexibility and more control over test execution.

As our test scripts so far are all in RSpec, we will use Rake, the de-facto build tool for Ruby. Rake is pre-bundled with the Ruby distribution. If you can run tests from command line, chances are that you already have had Rake installed.

I am going to show you some Rake build scripts. If you don't feel comfortable writing them, don't worry, as you don't have to write them. The build script that came with the sample project for this chapter (under sources/ch11) should work if your test scripts are in RSpec. I recommend that you download the sample project for this chapter from the book's web site.

The command below shows the defined tasks in a build script file (named Rakefile by default):

```
rake -T
```

The output below lists four tasks:

```
rake test:all         Run all tests from command line
rake test:ci          Run as part of CI build, reporting test results as ...
rake test:ordered     Run tests in smart execution order based on history...
rake test:selected    Run selected tests from command line
```

Run selected tests

The Rake task *test:selected* below will run the test cases from two test script files: *login_spec.rb* and *flight_spec.rb*:

```
RSpec::Core::RakeTask.new("test:selected") do |t|
  # list test script files you want to run below
  t.pattern = ["login_spec.rb","flight_spec.rb"]
end
```

Invoke the Rake task (in a command prompt for Windows users) by typing:

```
rake test:selected
```

The below is a sample output of executing 4 test cases in those 2 test script files. In this instance, all of them have passed ('.' means pass, 'F' means failed):

```
....

Finished in 29.796875 seconds

4 examples, 0 failures
```

Run all tests

Quite often you want to run all tests together (as in regression testing), including new ones that might have been added by your colleagues. Here is a Rake task definition to run all test script files ending with *_spec.rb* in the folder where *Rakefile* is.

```
RSpec::Core::RakeTask.new("test:all") do |t|
  t.spec_files = ["*_spec.rb"]
end
```

Invoke the Rake task:

```
rake test:all
```

The below is a sample output of executing 6 test cases with 1 failed:

```
....F.

1)
'Passenger Can enter passenger details (watir)' FAILED
expected: "Wendy Tester",
     got: "Bob Tester" (using ==)
./passenger_spec.rb:33:


Finished in 68.109375 seconds

6 examples, 1 failure
rake aborted!
```

With one line of commands (*rake test:all*), you can now effortless execute a series of tests. However, flexible execution is often enough, it lack of information and quick feedback, that's where the CI server comes in.

Set up a continuous testing server: BuildWise

Now we know how to invoke automated tests from build scripts, the next step is to get it run within a continuous build server. Some may feel overwhelmed by the sound of that. That's why I created BuildWise, a simple-to-use continuous build server designed for web test automation. I won't be able to cover full continuous integration (which is beyond the scope of testing) here, but I will show you how to set up a continuous testing server to manage your test executions better, a lot better.

You are probably getting used to my style by now. Yes, I will walk through an example to set up a continuous testing server. And we will do it within a few minutes.

To get CI working, we need a source control server. In this exercise, we will use Git (a popular distributed VCS). It this sounds complicated or lengthy, it isn't really. What's more, Git and BuildWise won't cost you a cent as it is free and open-source.

Objective

- Install the CI server BuildWise
- Create a BuildWise project for existing test scripts
- Trigger a test execution of all (or selected) test scripts with a click of a button
- See test execution results on the CI Server

Install BuildWise CI Server

For many, CI is a new concept. So, to boost your confidence, I will make the installation as simple as it can be. Just download and install BuildWise standalone windows installer (BuildWiseStandalone-X-setup.exe, there is also a buildwise-X.zip which can be installed on Unix and Mac) from the book site. Please do not change the default installation directory *C:\agileway\buildwise-standalone*, as it is referenced in the included sample test projects. Once you get familiar with BuildWise and CI, you are free to change.

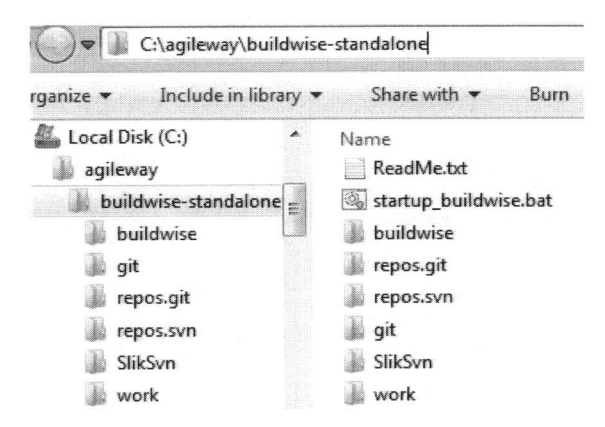

Contents of the *buildwise-standalone* folder:

- **Test scripts source controlled in a source control server**
  A test project *C:\agileway\buildwise-standalone\work\agiletravel-ui-tests*.
- **Source Control Client Software**
  Git client is located at: *C:\agileway\buildwise-standalone\git*.
- **BuildWise**
  BuildWise is located at *C:\agileway\buildwise-standalone\buildwise*.
- **Rakefile with test execution tasks**
  The sample project includes a Rakefile with necessary tasks defined.
- **The application (web site) under testing is up running**
  See the book site for the URL of this test web site.

Note: RubyShell[1] needs to be installed first. If you are using the standard Ruby Windows installer, you need to install all required RubyGems yourself, then BuildWise.

---
[1]http://testwisely.com/testwise/downloads

Start up BuildWise CI Server

- double click **start_buildwise.bat** under folder *C:\agileway\buildwise-standalone*
- open *http://localhost:3618* in your browser:

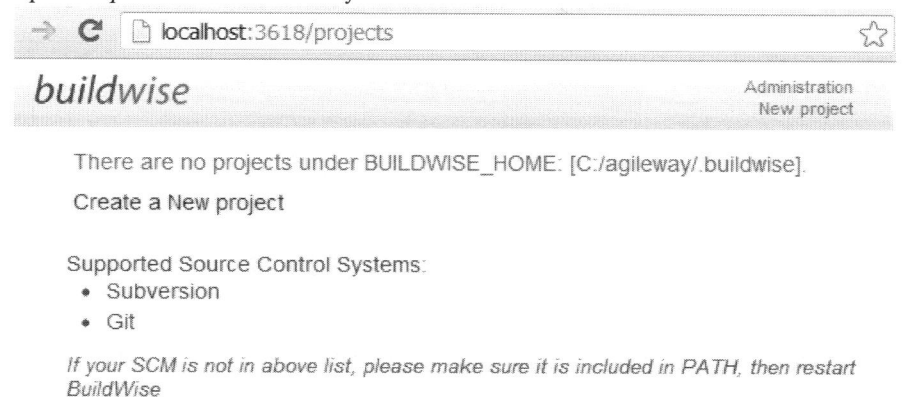

> There are no projects under BUILDWISE_HOME: [C:/agileway/.buildwise].
>
> Create a New project
>
> Supported Source Control Systems:
> - Subversion
> - Git
>
> *If your SCM is not in above list, please make sure it is included in PATH, then restart BuildWise*

Create BuildWise Project

BuildWise uses a concept of 'Project'. A quick way to create a project in BuildWise is providing a name (for display), an identifier, and a local working folder containing test scripts.

New project

Option 1. Loading from a working folder or Specify manually

Name:	AgileTravel UI Tests
Identifier:	agiletravel-ui-tests *(lower case and unique, e.g. adminwise_ui_tests)*
Working folder:	C:\agileway\buildwise-standalone\work\agiletravel-ui-tests
	(Specify the SCM checked out project folder on the machine running BuildWise server)
SCM User:	*(you may want to use dedicated user for CI)*
SCM Password:	
Project Template:	Continuous Test Server
UI test folder:	spec
	(where the UI tests are)
Rake Task for UI Tests:	test:ci
	(Next page will help you with Rakefile if you haven't had one)

[Create] [Cancel]

This will create the project *agiletravel-ui-tests* in BuildWise.

Trigger test execution manually

To start a build (for our purpose, 'Build' means execution of automated functional tests), click 'Build Now' button.

Agile Travel UI Tests
NEVER BUILT   [Build Now]

The colour of lava lamp (for the project) is now changed to orange, indicating a build is under the way.

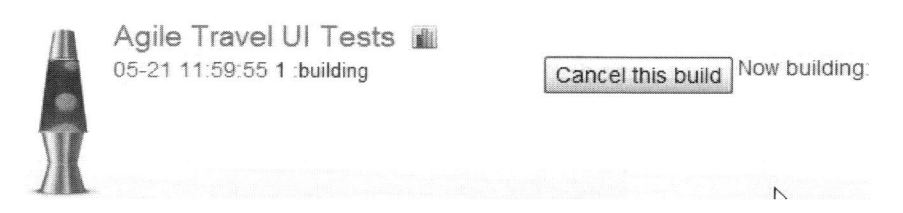

> **Agile Travel UI Tests**
> 05-21 11:59:55 1 :building
> [Cancel this build] Now building

Soon you will see an Internet Explorer window launching and your tests executing.

Feedback while test execution in progress

Click a build label (such as '1 :building') to show details of test execution:

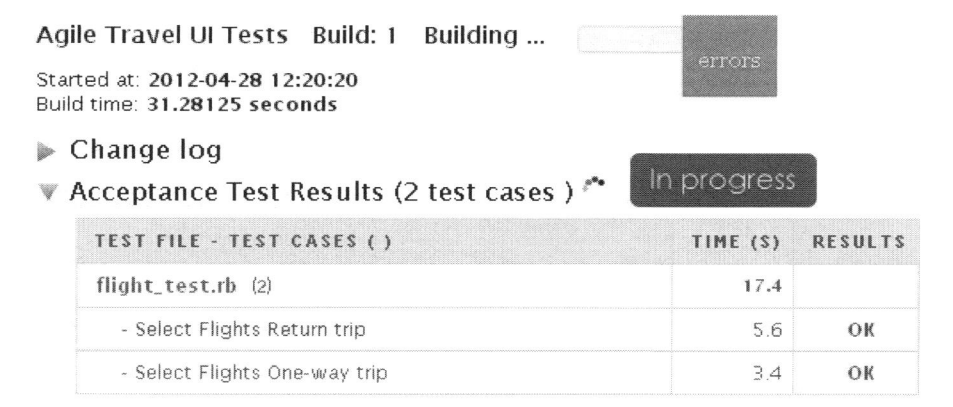

> **Agile Travel UI Tests   Build: 1   Building ...**
> Started at: **2012-04-28 12:20:20**
> Build time: **31.28125 seconds**
>
> ▶ Change log
> ▼ Acceptance Test Results (2 test cases)   [In progress]
>
> | TEST FILE - TEST CASES ( ) | TIME (S) | RESULTS |
> |---|---|---|
> | flight_test.rb (2) | 17.4 | |
> | - Select Flights Return trip | 5.6 | OK |
> | - Select Flights One-way trip | 3.4 | OK |

You can inspect test results of executed tests while other tests are still running. The above screenshot was taken when 2 (of 6) test cases in one test script file finished execution.

Inspect test failures

You can inspect test failures on BuildWise while a test execution is in progress.

Acceptance Test Results (6 test cases) | Export Excel , CSV

TEST FILE - TEST CASES (in 2 test scripts files)	TIME (S)	RESULTS
passenger_test.rb (1)	14.2	
- Passenger Can enter passenger details (watir)	7.8	Failure

```
expected: "Wendy Tester",
     got: "Bob Tester" (using ==) (Spec::Expectations::ExpectationNotMetError)
./passenger_test.rb:33
```

From the error or failure description, we can identify the cause. From line numbers in the error trace, we can easily navigate to the test case in a testing tool where the error occurred.

Please note that the tests are executed on the build server, not on your machine (unless you are running BuildWise locally). You can now open test cases in TestWise on your computer and run them, without waiting for the CI build to complete.

Build finished

When a test execution completes, you will get the full test results shown on BuildWise. You can even export them to an Excel spreadsheet. For the build below, only 1 has failed out of 6 automated test cases.

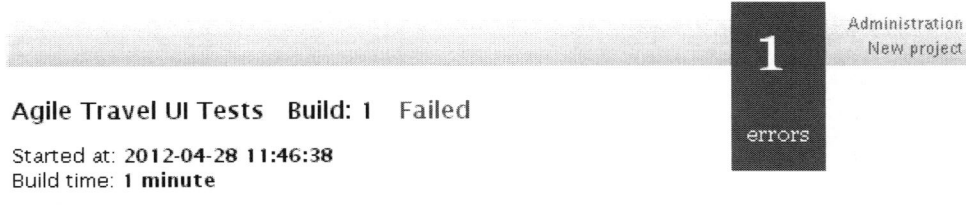

Administration
New project

1 errors

Agile Travel UI Tests   Build: 1   Failed

Started at: **2012-04-28 11:46:38**
Build time: **1 minute**

▶ **Build artifacts**
▶ **Change log**
▼ **Acceptance Test Results (6 test cases) | Export** Excel , CSV

TEST FILE - TEST CASES (in 4 test scripts files)	TIME (S)	RESULTS
passenger_test.rb (1)	14.2	
- Passenger Can enter passenger details (watir)	7.8	Failure

If you visit the home page of BuildWise server, a red lava lamp is shown next to the project.

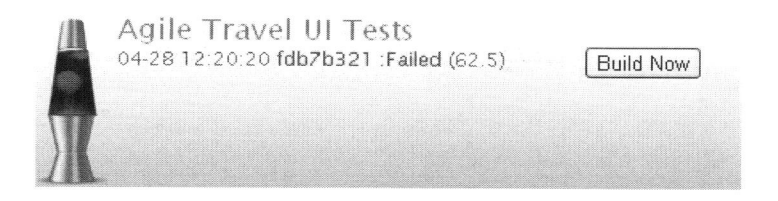

Fix the Build

Continuing our exercise, we want to fix the failed test. From the test failure trace, we can easily identify the failure occur at line 33 in *passenger_spec.rb*.

```
expect(text_field(:name, "holder_name").value).to eq("Wendy Tester")
```

After analyzing, the text in fact now should be 'Bob Tester'. So we correct the assertion

```
expect(text_field(:name, "holder_name").value).to eq("Bob Tester")
```

Commit the changes to the parent Git repository by running the following commands in a command window:

```
cd c:\agileway\buildwise-standalone\work\agiletravel-ui-tests
c:\agileway\buildwise-standalone\git\bin\git commit -a -m "fixed wrong asser\
tion in passenger_test"
c:\agileway\buildwise-standalone\git\bin\git push origin master
```

Now trigger another build. On the build report (see below), you can see a change log showing who changed what files at what time and the comment.

▼ Change log

```
        commit 4bc9b881d003a7398755469a72432ecf2e7220b2
Author: unknown
Date:   Sat Apr 28 12:43:17 2012 +1000

    fixed wrong assertion in passenger_test

 passenger_test.rb |    2 +-
 1 files changed, 1 insertions(+), 1 deletions(-)
```

> **Build trigger**
>
> We saw a manually triggered build. A build can also be triggered when a check-in occurs to the version control server. For example, if you added a new test script and checked it in to the VCS, a build will start momentarily to run all the tests including this newly added one. Refer to your CI server documentation for details.

Test Execution Order

BuildWise keeps a history of test execution results. Based on that knowledge, we can be a little smarter in setting the execution order of test scripts. For example, the sample build script tries to run the recently failed test cases first. The objective is to provide programmers and testers timely feedback on most likely to fail tests.

▶ Change log
▼ Acceptance Test Results (1 test cases)   *Running last failed tests first!*

TEST FILE - TEST CASES ( )	TIME (S)	RESULTS
passenger_test.rb (1)	9.9	
- Passenger Can enter passenger details (watir)	5.8	OK

▼ Build Log

In above build, the first executed test script file is *passenger_spec.rb*, the one failed in last build. Pretty neat, hey?

Success: Green Lamp

If all tests passed, you will be rewarded with a green lava lamp on the dashboard page.

Agile Travel UI Tests
04-28 12:43:38 4bc9b881 :OK (62.2)
04-28 12:20:20 fdb7b321 :Failed (62.5)

Notification

You can configure continuous integration servers to send notifications immediately after a build has finished. Email is the most common method. Here is one for a failed build:

```
From:    tester1@agileway.com.au                              Hide
Subject: [adminwise-ui-tests] Build still broken (36)          6
Date:    14 November 2011 9:39:28 PM AEST
To:      Zhimin Zhan , Zhimin@AgileWay Zhan

--
This email generated by BuildWise v0.3.35,
http://testwisely.com/en/buildwise
```

and one for a successful build:

```
From:    tester1@agileway.com.au                              Hide
Subject: [adminwise-ui-tests] Build fixed by (37)
Date:    14 November 2011 10:17:31 PM AEST
To:      Zhimin Zhan , Zhimin@AgileWay Zhan


@@@UI test@@@
C:/work/.buildwise/work/adminwise-ui-tests/sources Administrator$
rake test:ci
Check test order: adminwise-ui-tests
 [buildwise.rake] Posting to |http://localhost:3618/builds/begin|
 [Rake] new build id =>|12|
...............................

Finished in 312.5 seconds

33 examples, 0 failures
```

Review

It is not that hard, is it? If you have been developing RWebSpec or Watir or Selenium tests using RSpec syntax, getting your tests running in BuildWise shall be quite straight forward. You can apply BuildWise configuration and the build script (Rakefile) of this sample project to your project with little modification.

Dynamic Build Process

While the continuous testing server we just set up makes it easy to manage test executions, it does not reduce total execution time. In other words, if it takes 1 hour to run tests from the command line, it will be still 1 hour when executed in CI server.

To cut the execution time, one effective solution is to distribute tests to multiple build machines to run them in parallel. If you reach the point that parallel execution is needed, congratulations! you have done well. Distributed test execution is out of the scope of this book. But here I briefly share one approach I have used successfully in projects. I named it the "Dynamic Build Process".

In dynamic build process, there are two projects set up on a continuous build server : Quick Build and Full Build.

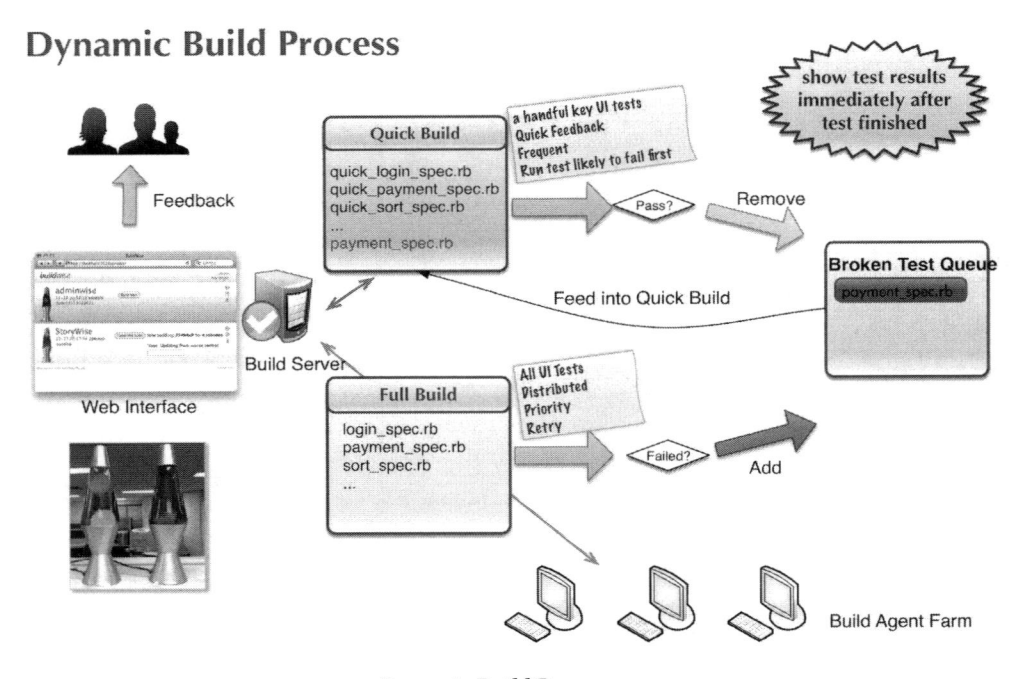

Dynamic Build Process

Quick Build runs a set of key tests on the build server, while Full Build runs all tests in parallel across multiple build machines. The purpose of Quick Build is to make sure key features in the system are still working as expected within a short period of time, usually under 10 minutes. A quick build is set to be triggered by a check-in to VCS, which means quick builds will run often, many times a day. Full build is usually scheduled to start before lunch and after work. Both full build and quick build can be triggered manually at any time.

The failed test cases from a recent full build will be added to the 'broken queue'. Next time when a quick build starts, it will run the tests in 'Broken queue' as well as the key tests. On receiving notifications of test failures, programmers and testers work together to analyse the cause and fix them. On new check-ins, a quick build starts again. If a test in 'broken queue' now passes in a quick build, it will be removed from the 'broken queue'. That way, the team will work on the feedback received from the CI server to fix all outstanding test failures, and get a green light!

12. Test Reporting

One benefit (besides many other) of test automation is that test results are report ready (after test execution, little effort required to get test report). In this chapter, we will look at how to use test results from automated test execution to help your test reporting.

Reporting Automated Test Results

Most of the testing frameworks support test execution from command line. This feature makes it easier to integrate with other systems, such as continuous integration servers. For executing a large number of tests, I too prefer running them from the command line over in testing IDEs. Based on the test results, I run failed tests in a testing IDE to debug.

RSpec by default reports test results in plain text like this:

```
User Login
- Sign in OK (FAILED - 1)
- Sign in failed (incorrect password)

Flight Finder
- Oneway Trip
- Return Trip

1)
'User Login Login OK' FAILED
expected "Register ..... " to include "Welcome Agileway"
./login_spec.rb:30:

Finished in 20.405858 seconds

4 examples, 1 failure
```

As you can see, the test report shows what you need to know about failed test cases, including

- test case name
- test script file
- brief error description
- line number where the error occurred

According to the report, you can open these tests in your testing tool to examine. I do this a lot (after checking test results from CI server).

RSpec also generates a colourful report in HTML by executing tests with *-fh* flag:

```
rspec -fh *_spec.rb > report.html
```

A sample RSpec HTML report (open report.html in a web browser):

While above test reports may be sufficient for internal use, you probably need a more flexible one for formal reporting purpose. The test result generated by JUnit, which started modern day unit testing, is in a structured XML format. By applying an XSLT (Extensible Stylesheet Language Transformations) or programming, you can transform test results in XML to other forms, such as this Excel spreadsheet:

	A	B	C	D	E	G	H
6	Total Test Cases:	4		Failed:	2	Time Cost:	33.625 secs
7							
8			Test Results				
9	Test File		Test Case			Result	Duration Seconds
10	login_spec.rb		Login failed (incorrect password)			F	0.578125
11	login_spec.rb		Login OK			F	1.09375
12	flighter_finder_spec.rb		Return Trip			P	5.203125
13	flighter_finder_spec.rb		Oneway Trip			P	26.75

Defect Tracking

Before we get on the topic, let me explain the term "Zero Bug Tolerance", that is, "zero tolerance" toward outstanding bugs. There is a dedicated section with title "Zero Bug Tolerance" in the 'Agile Testing' book [Crispin & Gregory 09], and 'The Agile of Agile Testing' book also has similar one: "No Bugs" [Shore & Warden 08].

If there is 'no bugs', therefore there is no need for defect tracking. For some testers who use defect tracking tools daily, this can be quite hard to comprehend. As Lisa Crispin and Janet Gregory pointed out "New agile teams usually have a hard time believing (zero bug tolerance) can be done." (Agile Testing, P418). They further added "The objective is not to get rid of a defect tracking system—it is to not need a defect tracking system. There is a big difference."

Defect tracking can be very counter-productive. That's why good agile teams try to avoid doing it. Defect tracking systems (DTS) separate testers and programmers, in a way. The time cost to read, update, disagree and argue (over classification of severity in particular) defects between different parties in a DTS could be huge. I have seen one defect print out from a DTS that was over 10 pages long.

People sometimes do things for the sake of doing it. For many software projects, in my opinion, defect tracking falls into this category. Let's explore further into the purpose of defect tracking. The common answers for this question "Why defect tracking is needed?" are:

- to have a record of error and the steps to replicate (for showing to the programmers)
- to prevent the same defect from appearing again

I agree with these objectives. However, they can be achieved without defect tracking. To let programmers know a defect is found, a tester can create an automated test to exhibit the error. The test case shall fail, of course. Then the tester checks into the source control and notify the programmers like *"run test case '123 password reset' to see an error on password reset in build 567 on the test server"*. By checking out from the SCM and running the test case, programmers can follow the steps to see the error on their screens, with little room for misunderstandings (as we know, people often get different ideas from the same text). Once this automated test is added to the regression test suite, which is executed several times a day as a part of the CI build process. This surely gives the team more assurance than the defect has been documented in the defect tracking system.

Having said that, defect tracking systems do provide value if test automation cannot be implemented well or there is a long feedback loop due to the nature of the project. I once worked in a project that had purchased a defect tracking system before I joined in. After the test automation and CI process were set up, the defect tracing system fell out of the team's focus quickly. During the project, the term 'defect tracking' was rarely mentioned.

How to achieve "Zero Bug Tolerance"? The answer is to embrace test automation as a team (here I mean a real team). Automated testing, especially as a part of continuous build process, provides the programmers quick feedback. Fixing newly found defects on a new build (from CI) is programmers' first priority. For obvious defects, programmers can check out the test scripts and run them to see the error on screen, then work on fixes to pass these tests. For tests that failed on valid application changes, testers go to update the test scripts. For ambiguous ones, whole team (customers, business analysts, testers and programmers) get together and analyse the cause, and the testers update the test scripts to reflect the agreement. With these updates being checked into source control, another build kicks off in CI server. At the end of day, the whole team is aiming for one or several good builds: without outstanding defects.

Requirement Traceability

> "I repeat, I have, in 30 years in the business, in industry, research and a little bit in government, NEVER seen a traceability matrix pays off." - Alistair Cockburn

Requirement Traceability refers to the ability to describe and follow the life of a requirement, in both a forward and backward direction. Management loves this stuff. Requirement traceability does offer value. However, as Alistair Cockburn pointed out, the question is at what cost (or whether it can be done).

In theory, the traceability shall be though all major phases of software life cycle.

Requirement → Design → Coding → Testing

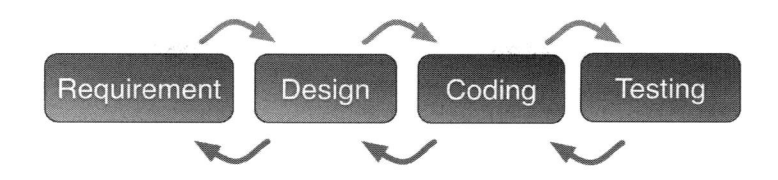

In reality, to achieve traceability to design and code is virtually impossible for enterprise applications. Once I joined a large project with a requirement traceability tool in place. The programmers were required to associate code changes to a requirement or change request before it could be checked into the source control server. It turned out that every one checked code against just one requirement: *Broken*. Programmers usually don't like spending long time searching for one requirement or change request before a code check-in, especially if they know it is going to be inaccurate and useless.

The only practical and feasible traceability is between requirements and functional tests.

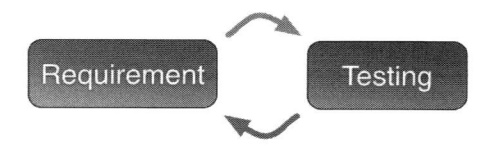

Requirement ↔ Testing

This makes sense too. Requirements are verified by functional tests and functional tests verify requirements. I have a reason for expressing the same meaning twice: traceability comes from two directions.

Traceability Matrix

An important document (or report) out of requirement traceability is the requirement traceability matrix which correlates requirements and tests in the form of a table. It is better explained with an example, here is the one from the "Traceability matrix" Wikipedia page.

Requirement Identifiers	Reqs Tested	REQ1 UC 1.1	REQ1 UC 1.2	REQ1 UC 1.3	REQ1 UC 2.1
Test Cases	321	3	2	3	1
Tested Implicitly	77				
1.1.1	1	x			
1.1.2	2		x	x	
1.1.3	2	x			
1.1.4	1			x	

Sample requirements traceability matrix

Please note that in above example test case "1.1.2" verifies the requirement UC 1.2 and 1.3, and requirement UC 1.1 is verified by test case 1.1.1 and 1.1.3. In other words, this is a many to many relationship.

Traceability with StoryWise

To illustrate the relation of automated tests and requirement traceability, I will use my opinionated solution: StoryWise. StoryWise extends Redmine, a popular free and open-source project management tool, with several modules. One of them is 'Requirement Traceability'.

To implement traceability for StoryWise, simply add requirement ids separated by commas and wrapped by "[ ]" in test case names (in RSpec test scripts).

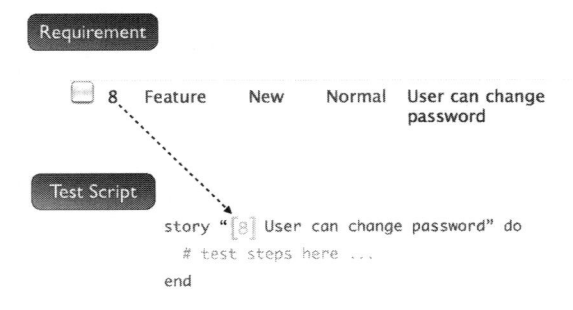

Add requirement traceability

Here is an example of one test case for two requirements:

```
story "[12, 23] User can ..." do
    ...
end
```

Then on the project setting page in StoryWise, specify a directory containing the latest automated functional test scripts files.

- **get requirement coverage (by automated functional tests)**

Click 'Refresh tests', StoryWise will scan and parse test scripts. After it is completed, you will be able to

- **get requirement coverage (by automated functional tests)**

- **show test scripts for a requirement**

Automated Test for 8 *'User can change password'*

1 test case for this user story.

1. File: *C:\work\adminwise\test\acceptance/profile_test.rb*

```
17    story "[8] User can change password" do
18      login_as("bob", "test")
19      click_link("Profile")
20      click_link("Change password")
21
22      password_change_page = expect_page PasswordChangePage
23      password_change_page.enter_current("password")
24      password_change_page.enter_new("newpass")
25      password_change_page.enter_confirm("newpass2")
26      password_change_page.click_button("Change")
27
28      page_text.should contain("Password doesn't match confirmation")
29      password_change_page.enter_confirm("newpass")
30      password_change_page.click_button("Change")
31
32      logout
33      login_as("bob", "newpass")
34      assert_link_present_with_text("Profile") # login Ok
35    end
```

- **generate requirement traceability matrix**

  Click the link

  View Traceability Matrix

  You will get a requirement traceability matrix in Excel

	A	B	C	D	E	F	G
1	**Requirement Traceability Matrix**						
2							
3	**AgileWay**					: 12/02/2012 18:17:59	
4							
5	Requirement test coverage:	96%			*Coverage Rate*		
6	User Story count:	33					
7	Test script files count:	14					
8	Test case count:	33					
9							
10	IDs	REQ 1	REQ 5	REQ 6	REQ 7	REQ 8	REQ 9
11	TC 1: "[1] A registered user can login"	X					
12	TC 2: "[27] Admin user can login"						
13	TC 3: "[28] Anonymous user cannot login - invalid p			*This requirement not covered*			
14	TC 4: "[29] Anonymous user cannot login - try go th						
15	TC 5: "[37] Create a new Todo list"						
16	TC 6: "[38] Can edit a Todo list name"			*Req #8 covered by TC #9*			
17	TC 7: "[39] Can add a new task in existing todo list"						
18	TC 8: "[40] Can delete Todo list"						
19	TC 9: "[8] User can change password"					X	
20	TC 10: "[24] Admin User can add a professional"						

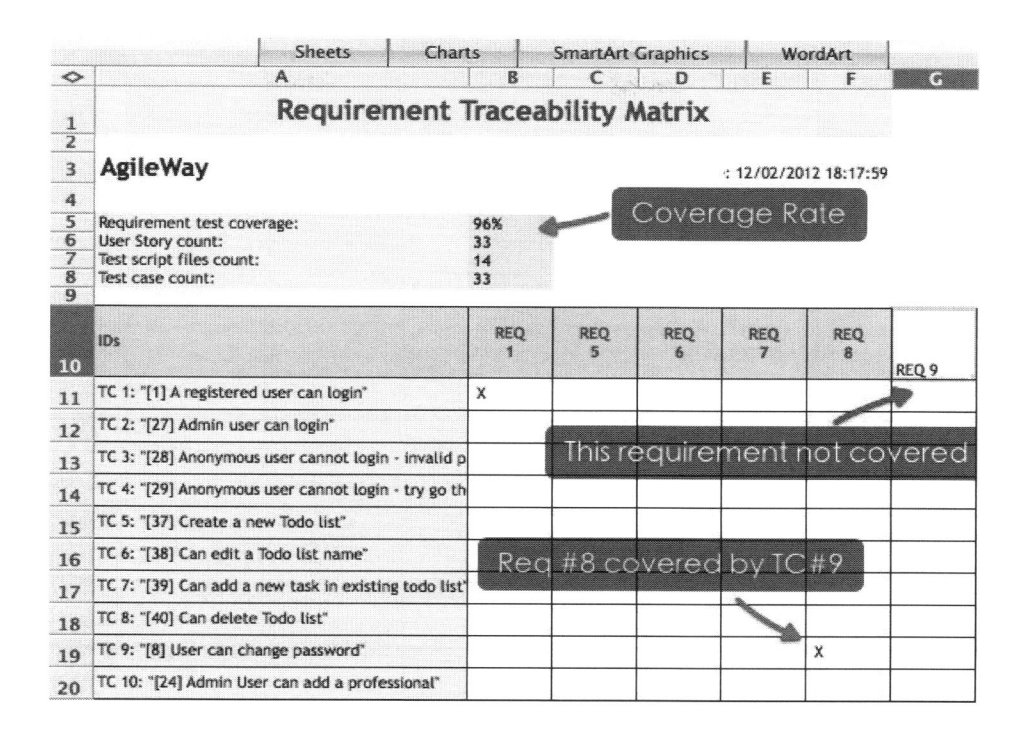

13. Selenium

So far we have been focusing on the Watir (RWebSpec) test framework and executing tests in Internet Explorer. Among the alternatives, Selenium is a more popular web test framework (My market research, searching 'selenium' on job seeking site, shows that Selenium is the most demanded skills for tech testers, at least in US and Australia). Even you are a die-hard Watir user, I still suggest you have a look at Selenium, as it supports multiple browsers (such as Firefox and Chrome) and multiple platforms (such as Linux and Mac). In this chapter, we will write tests in Selenium with the same techniques learned.

Selenium Framework

Selenium, also known as Selenium-WebDriver, is a free open-source web test framework that supports multiple browsers on multiple platforms with multiple language support. In the exercises below, I will use Selenium-WebDriver's Ruby language binding for two reasons: it is a script language and you already know it. Also, it is not hard to convert Selenium tests in Ruby to another language.

Selenium-WebDriver was released in July 2011. From my observation, there was a lack of reliability in its early releases, particularly in IE (FireFox is best supported). However, this project is actively being developed and a new release comes out every week or two, and it is noticeably getting better. I have no doubt it will be the mainstream web test framework.

Selenium IDE

Selenium includes an official recorder-and-playback tool: Selenium IDE.

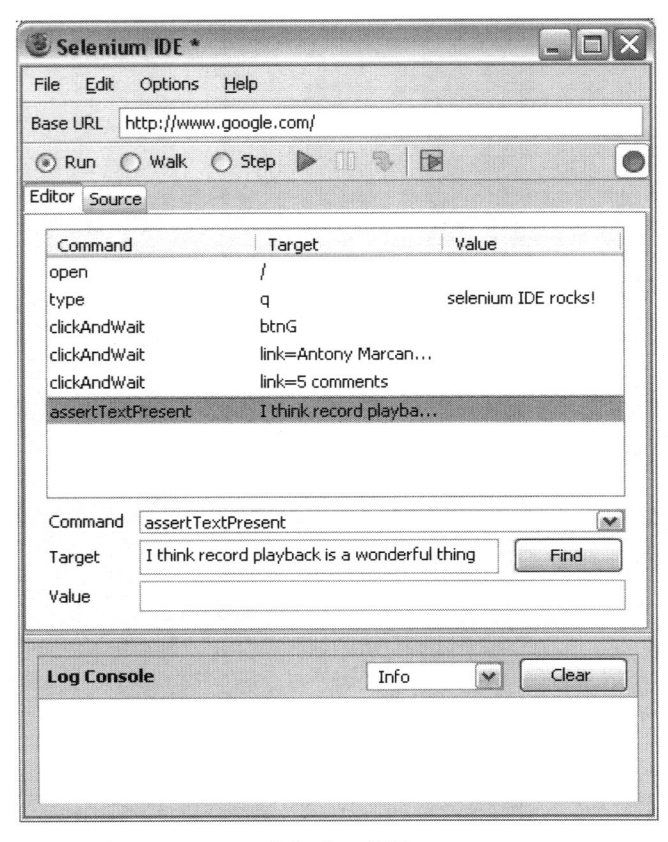

Selenium IDE

Selenium IDE is a Firefox extension. Besides recording (and playing back) function, it supports editing and debugging tests. However, these extra features (playback, edit and debug) keep me from using it. In my highly subjective view, recorders should just do the recording test steps, nothing else. Recorded test scripts are not meant for real use, testers need to refine them. Tools such as Selenium IDE are helpful, but may give testers, especially newcomers, a false impression of test automation. Jason Huggins, the creator of original Selenium, said "Record/playback testing tools should be clearly labeled as 'training wheels'" [AAFTT 09]. I certainly agree on this.

Some readers might have observed that the TestWise Recorder has a tab named 'Selenium-WebDriver', where you can find recorded test scripts in Selenium-WebDriver syntax.

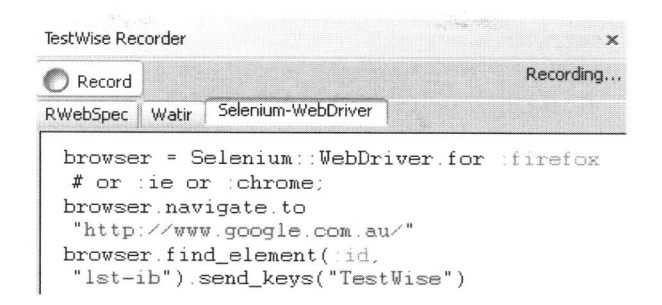

```
TestWise Recorder                              x
  ◯ Record                             Recording...
  RWebSpec │ Watir │ Selenium-WebDriver
    browser = Selenium::WebDriver.for :firefox
    # or :ie or :chrome;
    browser.navigate.to
     "http://www.google.com.au/"
    browser.find_element(:id,
     "lst-ib").send_keys("TestWise")
```

In the chapter, I will continue to use TestWise Recorder for the exercises.

Selenium Syntax

This is not a tutorial for Selenium, as you can easily find one on Internet. Instead, I am trying to leverage what you have learned to get into Selenium quickly. Let's firstly look at a simple Selenium test: Google Image Search

```
require "selenium-webdriver"

driver = Selenium::WebDriver.for :firefox
driver.navigate.to "http://google.com"

driver.find_element(:id, "gb_2").click # Click Images link
element = driver.find_element(:name, 'q')
element.send_keys "Camel"
element.submit #submit the search form
```

Compared to Watir, Selenium uses a generic *find_element* to identify a web control with one of the attributes below:

- :id
- :link_text
- :link
- :partial_link_text
- :name
- :tag_name
- :xpath

- :class
- :class_name
- :css

Typical operations that a web control can perform include:

- click
- clear
- send_keys

Case Study: Switch RWebSpec to use Selenium

RWebSpec in fact is a wrapper (from v4) for both Watir and Selenium. In this exercise, we will switch the web test driver (Watir ⇒ Selenium) in RWebSpec test scripts and run them against Firefox, IE and Chrome.

Prerequisites

- **Existing RWebSpec Project**

    At the end of Chapter 8, I asked you to do a exercise: apply refactorings to 6 test cases we created in Chapter 5. If you haven't done it, I included mine under *ch08-refactoring\refactor_case_study*.

- **TestWise Community Edition**

    For readers who are using their favourite IDE/editors, don't worry, I will show you how to execute tests from the command line (I am sure you can figure out how to do it with your tool from my examples)

- **Ruby runtime and selenium-webdriver gem installed** (for executing tests from the command line)

    For Windows users, you need to install RubyShell[1], if you haven't already done do.

Convert

Clone your working project from the Ch08 exercise (or copy from the sample source).

---

[1] http://testwisely.com/testwise/downloads

Execute tests in TestWise

Open the test project in TestWise. Open the project setting, select 'Selenium-WebDriver' as the web automation driver (leave 'RWebSpec' as test script syntax).

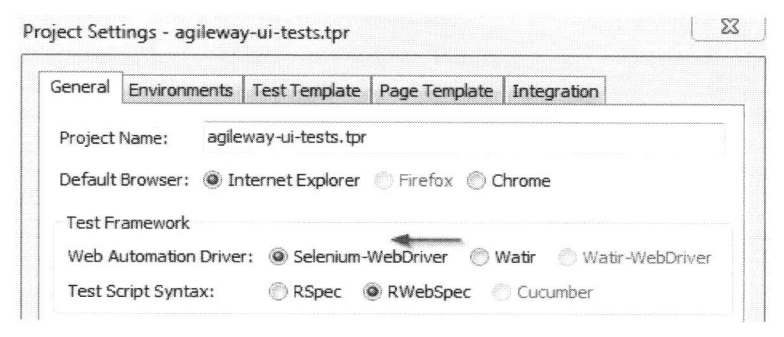

Select Selenium as Web Automation Driver

Execute tests from command line or other tools

Add the following line in *test_helper.rb* in the new project:

```
RWebSpec.framework = "Selenium-WebDriver"
```

You are now ready to run tests using Selenium against Chrome and Firefox.

Run in Firefox

In TestWise, select the test script file *flight_spec.rb* and then select Firefox (see below). Then click ▶ on the toolbar.

Select Firefox

You should see a Firefox window pop up in a few seconds and the test being executed in it.

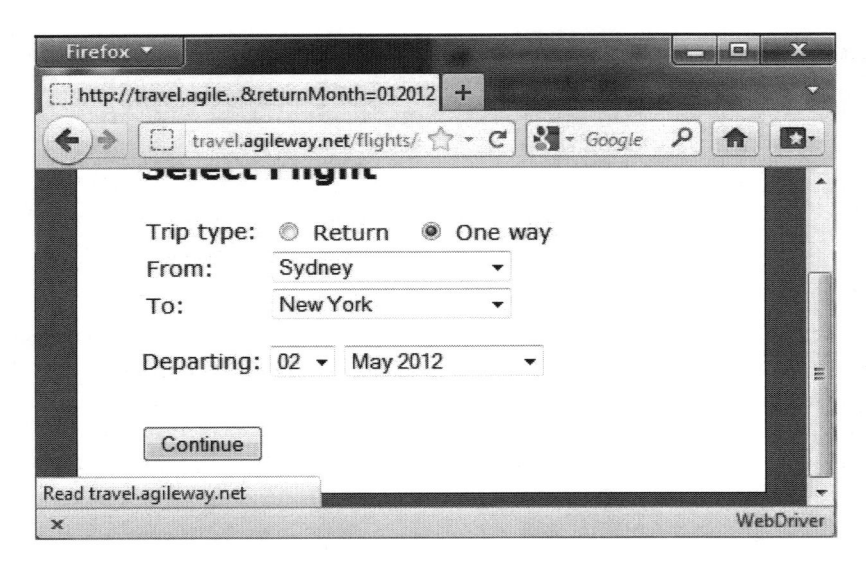

The text 'WebDriver' at the right bottom corner indicates that this is a Firefox browser window started by Selenium.

The *flight_spec.rb* should pass. If there were test steps written in Watir, it won't work here. For example, in *passenger_spec.rb*, we had one assertion in Watir:

```
expect(text_field(:name, "holder_name").value).to eq("Bob Tester")
```

This is to verify the value of card holder's name in the text box is "Bob Tester"

We can make the assertion work in Selenium by changing it to:

```
expect(text_field(:name, "holder_name").value).to eq("Bob Tester")
```

Run from command line

In test_helper.rb, add the following line:

```
$TESTWISE_BROWSER = "Firefox"
```

Then type the command below in a command line window to run one test script file:

```
rspec flight_spec.rb
```

Run in Google Chrome

To run tests in Google Chrome, besides the Chrome browser itself, *chromedriver* also needs to be installed. If you haven't done so, the error message gives clear instructions: "Unable to find the *chromedriver* executable. Please download the server from https://sites.google.com/a/chromium.org/chromedriver and place it somewhere on your PATH."

In TestWise (Professional Edition), select browser Chrome on the toolbar and run, the tests will be executed in a Google Chrome browser.

Run from command line

In test_helper.rb, add (or change to) the following line:

```
$TESTWISE_BROWSER = "Chrome"
```

Then type the command below in a command line window to run all test script files:

```
rspec *_spec.rb
```

Run in IE

We can also run the tests in Internet Explorer by selecting IE icon on the toolbar in TestWise:

Select browser IE

When a tests starts to execute in IE, before navigating the target test site, you will see this first:

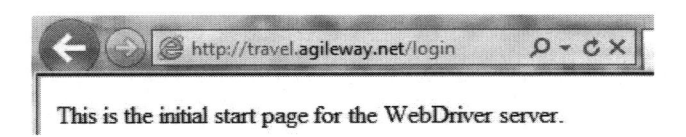

This is the initial start page for the WebDriver server.

If you get this on IE9: "Unexpected error launching Internet Explorer. Protected Mode must be set to the same value (enabled or disabled) for all zones." Go to 'Internet Options', select each zone (as illustrated below) and make sure they are all set to the same mode (protected or not).

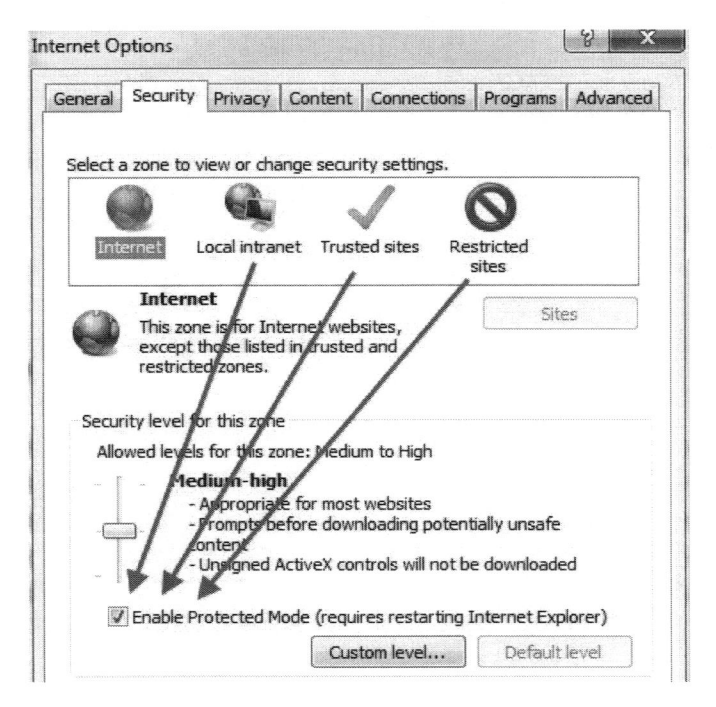

Further configuration is required for IE10 and IE11, see IE and IEDriverServer Runtime Configuration[2] for details.

Run from command line

In test_helper.rb, add (or change to) the following line:

```
$TESTWISE_BROWSER = "IE"
```

[2]https://code.google.com/p/selenium/wiki/InternetExplorerDriver#Required_Configuration

Then type the command below in a command line window to run two tests with test results in :

```
rspec -fh flight_spec.rb passenger_spec.rb > output.html
```

Review

It seemed that we hardly changed the test scripts (all we did was copying them over) and they now are running in different browsers. Just like RWebSpec to Watir, we can use selenium-webdriver syntax directly in RWebspec as well.

```
click_link("Home") # rwebspec
find_element(:link_text, "Sign off").click # selenium-webdriver
```

Run in Firefox on Mac

The above tests can also be executed against Firefox and Chrome on Mac. You can try them with TestWise Mac edition.

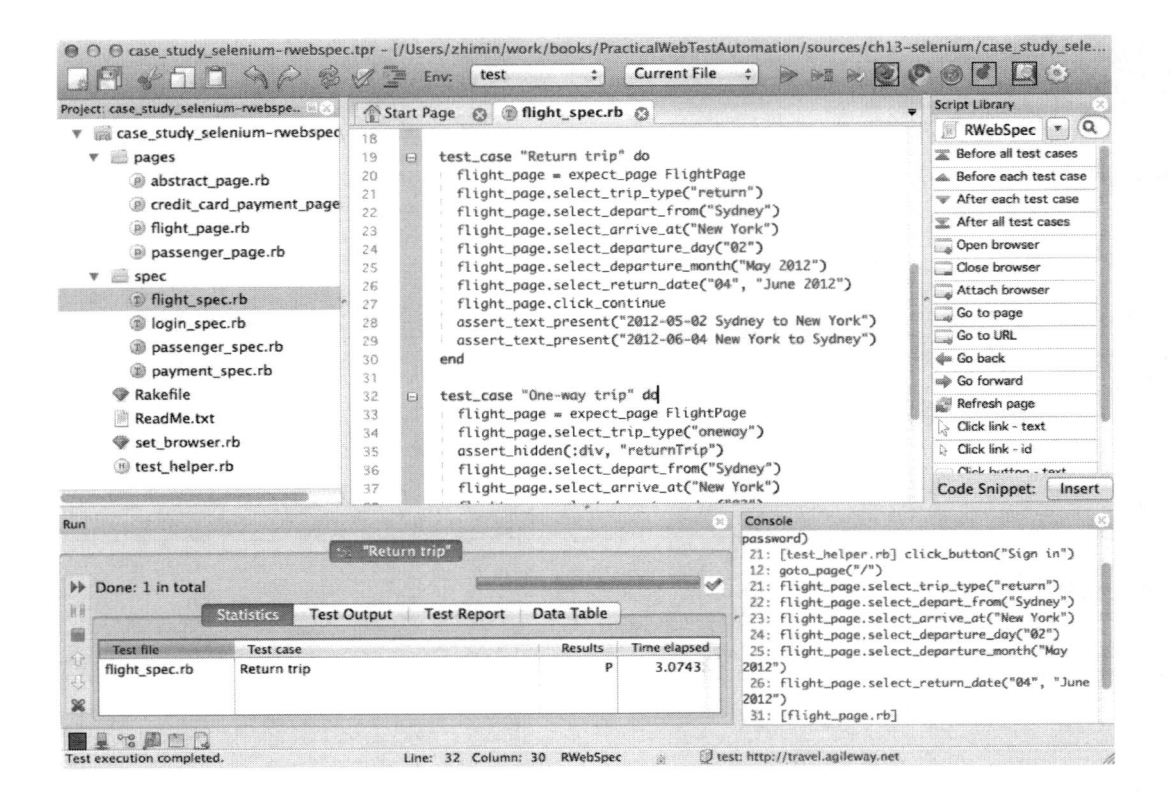

Case Study: Selenium-WebDriver and RSpec

In the previous exercise, we got the tests running in different browsers by using Selenium as the engine underneath. You might not feel that you are learning Selenium as the test scripts are pretty much the same. This is particularly convenient for people who want to switch the web test driver between Watir and Selenium-WebDriver. However, I know some of you want to learn how to write real (or shall I say: raw) Selenium tests.

In this exercise, we will write 6 tests for Agile Travel site (again) using Selenium directly with RSpec. Instead of starting from scratch (as in Chapter 5), I want to use the existing test scripts in *ch08-refactoring\refactor_case_study*. Obviously the test steps (in RWebSpec) won't work here, they need to be replaced with raw Selenium-WebDriver test steps. Our design: reusable functions in test_helper and the use of page classes remains valid.

This exercise may be a bit long and complex. Don't worry, you can find the final working sources under *ch13-selenium\case_study-selenium-rspec*. The screencasts on the web site will offer some help too.

Here we go:

1. **Create new test project**

   ![New Project dialog]

   Note the test script syntax is now set to *RSpec*.

2. **Copy test and page classes and functions in test helper**
   Copy the following files from ch08-refactoring\refactor_case_study to the new project folder:
   - spec/*_spec.rb
   - pages/credit_card_payment_page.rb
   - pages/flight_page.rb
   - pages/passenger_page.rb

   And copy the two functions (*sign_in* and *sign_off*) in *ch08-refactoring\refactor_case_study\test_helper.rb* to the *test_helper.rb* in the new project:

```
def sign_in(username, password)
  enter_text("username", username)
  enter_text("password", password)
  click_button("Sign in")
end

def sign_off
  click_link("Sign off")
end
```

3. **Change RWebSpec to RSpec: keywords**

   RWebSpec extends RSpec with some keywords for defining test suite and test cases, such as **test_case** and **story**. Now we need to restore to standard RSpec keywords: **it** (beginnings of test cases).

   for example:

   ```
   test_case "User can sign in OK" do
   ```

   to

   ```
   it "User can sign in OK" do
   ```

   A fast way to do it in TestWise is to use 'Replace in Project' (select menu 'Search' -> 'Replace in Project')

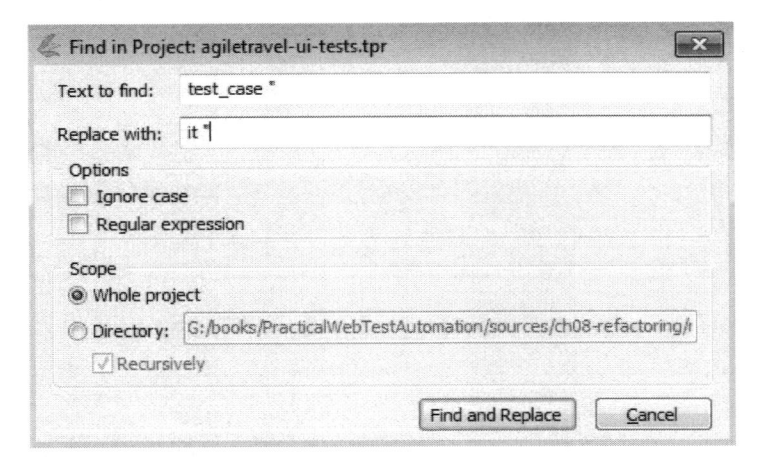

   Click 'Find and Replace'

```
Find
  Replace All    Replace Selected    Collapse All
  Replace
    'test_case "'
    'it "'
  Found 6 occurrences in 4 files
    spec/login_spec.rb
      14: test_case "User can sign in OK" do
      20: test_case "User failed to sign in due to invalid password" do
    spec/payment_spec.rb
      15: test_case "Get booking confirmation after payment " do
```

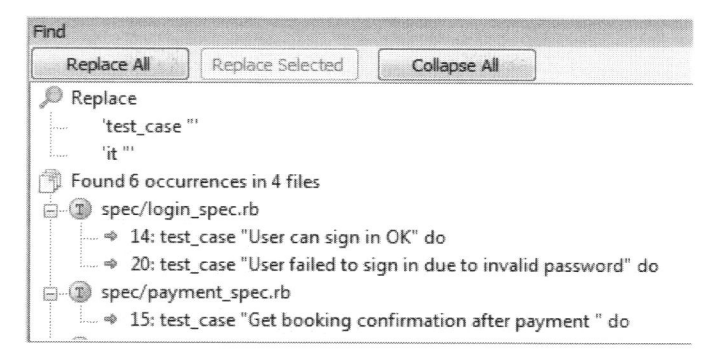

Then click 'Replace All' button, and select menu 'File' -> 'Save All' to save the changes.

4. **Change RWebSpec to Selenium: launch and close browser**

   open_browser is a convenient function defined in RWebSpec to start a new browser window or reuse an existing one. We need to change

   ```
   before(:all) do
     open_browser
     #...
   end
   ```

   to

   ```
   before(:all) do
     @browser = Selenium::WebDriver.for(:firefox)  # or :chrome, :ie
     @browser.navigate.to("http://travel.agileway.net")
     ...
   end
   ```

   Also we need to change

   ```
   close_browser
   ```

   to

   ```
   @browser.quit
   ```

   For impatient readers, you may run the test and will see a Firefox browser starting up. Astute readers will notice the browser and environment selection in TestWise does't work any more. That is because *open_browser* in RWebSpec does all that for us, but don't worry, we can achieve the same by changing the open browser test statement to:

```ruby
before(:all) do
  @browser = Selenium::WebDriver.for(the_browser)
  @browser.navigate.to(site_url)
  # ...
end
```

the_browser and *site_url* are two functions defined in *test_helper.rb*. *the_browser* sets the browser type based on the browser selection on TestWise toolbar; *site_url* sets the web site root URL based on the target server selection in TestWise.

```ruby
def the_browser
  if $TESTWISE_BROWSER then
    $TESTWISE_BROWSER.downcase.to_sym
  else
    RUBY_PLATFORM =~ /mingw/ ? "ie".to_sym : "firefox".to_sym
  end
end

def site_url(default = "http://travel.agileway.net")
  $TESTWISE_PROJECT_BASE_URL || default
end
```

The implementation of these 2 functions are TestWise specific, it shall be quite easy to change them for your testing tool.

5. **Change RWebSpec to Selenium: functions**

    If we run the 'User can sign in OK' test now, a Firefox window will start up and open Agile Travel site correctly, but failed immediately. Examine the test output:

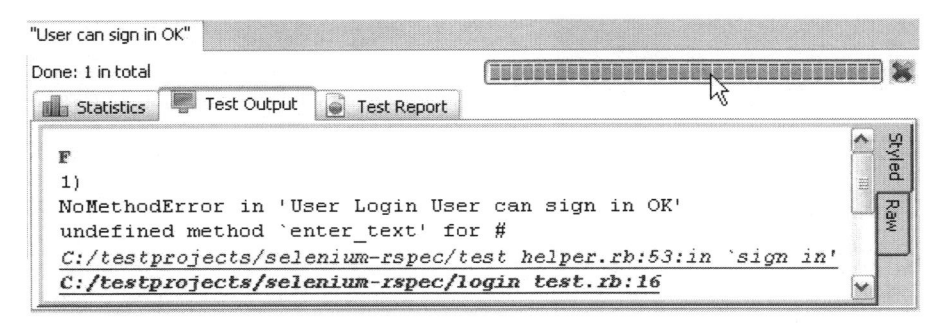

```
F
1)
NoMethodError in 'User Login User can sign in OK'
undefined method `enter_text' for #
C:/testprojects/selenium-rspec/test_helper.rb:53:in `sign_in'
C:/testprojects/selenium-rspec/login_test.rb:16
```

We see in *sign_in* function in test_helper.rb, it still uses RWebSpec syntax. Open a new Firefox window and enable TestWise Recorder to record sign in operations.

```
browser.find_element(:id,
 "username").send_keys("agileway")
browser.find_element(:id,
 "password").send_keys("testwise")
browser.find_element(:xpath,"//input[@value='Sign
 in']").click
```

Replace test steps in *sign_in* function with recorded test steps, and pre-append '@' in the front of 'browser.' (to access @browser instance variable defined in test script file).

```
def sign_in(username, password)
    @browser.find_element(:id, "username").send_keys("agileway")
    @browser.find_element(:id, "password").send_keys("test")
    @browser.find_element(:xpath,"//input[@value='Sign in']").click
end
```

6. **Change RWebSpec to Selenium: Assertion**

Run the test again, This time, we can see the username and password were entered, but failed on assertion step.

```
15      it "User can sign in OK" do
16        sign_in("agileway", "test")
17        assert_text_present("Welcome agileway")
18        sign_off
19      end
```

This is because *assert_text_present* is a RWebSpec function. We need to use a generic RSpec assertion. The current version Selenium-WebDriver (as of 2012-11) does not support the text view of browser, so we need to use raw page source for verification.

```
<div id="user_nav">
    Welcome <b>agileway</b>
```

So we change to

```
it "User can sign in OK" do
  sign_in("agileway", "testwise")
  expect(@browser.page_source).to include("Welcome <b>agileway</b>")
  sign_off
end
```

While we are here, we know **sign_off** function defined in *test_helper.rb* is still in RWebSpec. This time, I am not going to use recorder.

Type `@browser.sfe` under `click_link("Sign off")`

```
def sign_off
  click_link("Sign off")
  @browser.sfe
end
```

press the Tab key, the 'sfe' snippet will be expanded to:

```
@browser.find_element(:how, "what")
```

Then type over 'link_text', press Tab key, type 'Sign off' and append '.click' in the end. Delete 'click_link("Sign off")', our *sign_off* function now becomes:

```
def sign_off
  @browser.find_element(:link_text, "Sign off").click
end
```

Rerun the test case "User can sign in OK" in *login_spec.rb*. The test now passed!

7. **Change RWebSpec to Selenium: test steps in page classes**

Now we switch our attention to "Can enter passenger details" test case in *passenger_spec.rb* which uses page classes.

Under "flight_page = expect_page FlightPage", type "ep", press Tab key

```
flight_page = expect_page FlightPage
expect_page |
flight_page.  ⓟ AbstractPage
flight_page.
flight_page.  ⓟ CreditCardPaymentPage
flight_page.
flight_page.  ⓟ FlightPage
flight_page.  ⓟ PassengerPage
```

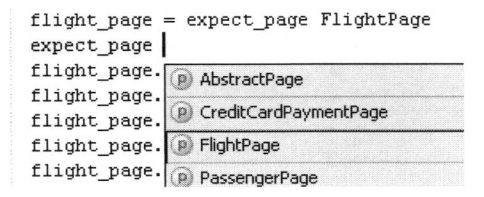

Select 'FlightPage', we get

```
flight_page = FlightPage.new(@browser)
```

Delete line with text `flight_page = expect_page FlightPage`.

Repeat replacements in the same way for `expect_page PassengerPage` and `expect_page CreditCardPaymentPage`

We knew this test case would fail if we ran it again as we haven't converted those test steps in page classes to Selenium yet. We can use the recorder to help on this. Start a new Firefox browser window with TestWise Recorder enabled, then sign in and navigate to the passenger page. Copy recorded test scripts (under Selenium-WebDriver tab, they are quite lengthy), paste into corresponding page classes and replace existing test steps with them one by one.

Let's take the test step (in `FlightPage`) for the selecting trip type as an example, Here is the RWebSpec version of `FlightPage`:

```
class FlightPage < AbstractPage
  #...
  def select_trip_type(trip_type)
    click_radio_option("tripType", trip_type) # RWebSpec
  end
```

By using the recorder, we get the test step in Selenium-WebDriver:

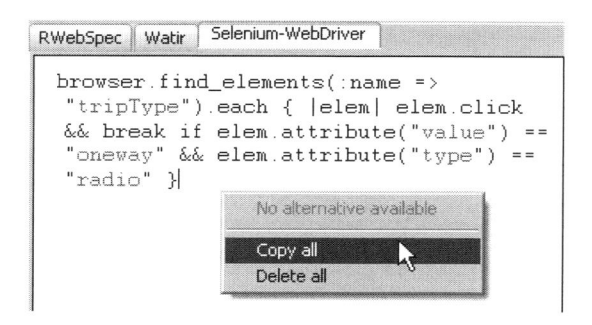

```
browser.find_elements(:name =>
 "tripType").each { |elem| elem.click
 && break if elem.attribute("value") ==
 "oneway" && elem.attribute("type") ==
 "radio" }|
```

No alternative available
Copy all
Delete all

Now paste the copied test step to overwrite its RWebSpec counterpart and change the radio option 'tripType' to the parameter 'trip_type'. We get:

```ruby
class FlightPage < AbstractPage
  #...
  def select_trip_type(trip_type)
    browser.find_elements(:name => "tripType").each { |elem|
      elem.click && break if elem.attribute("value") == trip_type &&
        elem.attribute("type") == "radio"
    }
  end
  #...
```

8. **Change RWebSpec to Selenium: AJAX**

   If you remember, there is a check for an AJAX operation: verifying the booking number present after payment being processed. Here is the assertion statement in RWebSpec:

   ```ruby
   try_for(15) { assert_text_present("Booking number")}
   ```

   Here is a similar one in Selenium-WebDriver:

   ```ruby
   wait = Selenium::WebDriver::Wait.new(:timeout => 15) # seconds
   wait.until { @browser.page_source.include?("Booking number") }
   ```

Now run *payment_spec.rb*, and it will pass!

Review

If you run test cases in *flight_spec.rb* and *passenger_spec.rb*, you may find they almost passed except the checks, which can be easily updated. Why? Because we have already updated functions in *test_helper*, *FlightPage* and *PassengerPage* classes when working on *payment_-spec.rb*.

The main purpose of this exercise is to show you that if test cases are designed well, updates are mostly only required for functions and page classes. For example, if you have 10,000 test cases use 100 page classes, when application changes, you are supposed to modify test steps in these 100 page classes rather than 10,000 test cases.

Cross Browser Functional Testing

I observed emerging interests in Cross-Browser Functional Testing by talking to candidates at software testing conference recently. This should not come to a surprise, as now the browser market is more diversified (based on the median stats on Wikipedia, the usage share in September 2011 for Firefox and Chrome are 25.0% and 20.9% respectively). Web application developers want their web sites to work in all major leading browsers, not just in IE. But question is how to verify that?

Though executing the same set of automated tests against different browsers is the ideal solution, it is very hard to implement. To keep a good suite of automated tests running against IE is not an easy task, let alone multiple browsers on different platforms. Even for a good framework such as Selenium-WebDriver, there are different behaviours on different browsers. For example, in *login_spec.rb*, we use the assertion below:

```
expect(@browser.page_source).to include("Welcome <b>agileway</b>")
```

However, the above test statement does not work for IE, as the *@browser.page_source* returned from IE and Firefox are different:

Internet Explorer 8	**Firefox 8**
`Welcome <B>agileway</B>`	`Welcome <b>agileway</b>`

If the project is determined to do full cross-browser functional testing, the cost and effort should be taken consideration. My advice: focus on one browser and get test automation running healthily, then gradually add tests to a key test suite (covering core business functions), which is executed against multiple browsers.

Comparison: Selenium and Watir

Unavoidably, people will ask the question: "Which one is better: Watir or Selenium?" Personally, I like Watir more for the reasons below:

- **More consistent and predictable syntax**

    Watir test steps mostly follow the same pattern, and usually within one line. To illustrate the difference between Watir and WebDriver, take a look at this simple test: select an option in a drop down list, here is the Watir version:

    ```
    browser = Watir::Browser.start "http://testwisely.com/demo/netbank"
    browser.select_list(:name, "account").select("Cheque")
    ```

    and in Selenium-WebDriver:

```
driver = Selenium::WebDriver.for :firefox
driver.get "http://testwisely.com/demo/netbank"
select_control = driver.find_element(:name, "account")
Selenium::WebDriver::Support::Select.new(select_control).select_by(:text, "C\
heque")
```

- **Faster**

    Here are the benchmark of executing the same test suite (our familiar 6 test cases) in two frameworks:

Watir (IE8):	24.4 seconds
Selenium-WebDriver (Firefox 8):	73.1 seconds

- **Reuse of the existing browser window**

    With Watir, we can write many tests against the currently opened browser window (the default behaviour for RWebSpec). One direct benefit is speed, as there is no need to start and close a browser for executing each test script file.

    Also it is possible to select specific test steps to run against current Internet Explorer window:

    ```
    browser.select_list(:id, "returnDay").set("07")
    browser.select_list(:id, "returnMonth").set("April 2012")
    browser.button(:value,"Continue").click
    ```

    Run "Can enter passenger details (watir..."   Ctrl+Shift+F10
    Run test cases in 'passenger_test.rb'   Shift+F10
    Run Selected Scripts Against Current Browser

    Which I found very handy during the development of an automated test case. I use this TestWise feature a lot. TestWise supports this feature for Selenium as well, with one minor restriction: it can only attach to the browser window started by the tests executed from TestWise.

- **Only supports Ruby**

    Watir comes with only one language syntax: Ruby. Some may argue this is a Watir's limitation, which I disagree. Experience tells me that more choices is not always a good thing. The 'r' in Watir is there for a reason: Ruby was chosen because it is suitable to write good test scripts, and it is enjoyable to use.

Watir's limitation is obvious: it only supports Internet Explorer. If you really to want to write tests in Watir and run them in Firefox and Chrome, you may consider watir-webdriver.

Watir-WebDriver is a Watir implementation built on WebDriver, it is written by Jari Bakken who brought us the ruby binding for Selenium-WebDriver.

14. Cucumber

So far I have covered two web test drivers Watir and Selenium-WebDriver, and one test framework RSpec. In this chapter, I will introduce another free and open-source test framework: Cucumber.

Cucumber Framework

Cucumber is a tool for running automated acceptance tests written in a behaviour driven development (BDD) style [Wikipedia]. Like RSpec, it is free, open-source and written in Ruby language. We have seen that tests in RSpec are quite readable, especially with the use of functions and page objects. Cucumber extends readability in execution specification even further: by means of its plain text approach. Let's look at this sample cucumber test (also called feature):

```
Scenario: The user should be able to change their password
   Given I have a signed in user "agileway" with "testwise"
   When I am on the change password page
   And I fill in current password with "test"
   And I fill in new password and confirmation with "newpass"
   When I press "Update"
   Then I should see "Your password updated successfully"
```

You can see it looks more like a structured English paragraph rather than a test script. How can this work? For each step (starts with *Given*, *And*, *When* and *Then*) of a scenario in a cucumber feature file, there is a corresponding step definition. Here are sample (empty) step definitions for the above cucumber test:

```
Given /^I have a signed in user "(.*?)" with "(.*?)"$/ do |arg1, arg2|
  pending # express the regexp above with the code you wish you had
end

When /^I am on the change password page$/ do
  pending # express the regexp above with the code you wish you had
end

When /^I fill in current password with "(.*?)"$/ do |arg1|
  pending # express the regexp above with the code you wish you had
end

When /^I fill in new password and confirmation with "(.*?)"$/ do |arg1|
  pending # express the regexp above with the code you wish you had
end

When /^I press "(.*?)"$/ do |arg1|
  pending # express the regexp above with the code you wish you had
end

Then /^I should see "(.*?)"$/ do |arg1|
  pending # express the regexp above with the code you wish you had
end
```

As you can see, step definitions tell Cucumber what to do when interpreting a particular step. The unusual characters such as "/^" and "(.*?)"$/" are regular expressions, a standard text matching syntax used in programming. By using testing tools supporting Cucumber such as TestWise, you don't need to know regular expressions to get started. However it will be helpful to know regular expressions if you are going to work with Cucumber a lot.

Case Study: Selenium and Cucumber

Cucumber can work with any Ruby-based frameworks such as Watir and Selenium-WebDriver. In this case study, I will use Selenium-WebDriver with Cucumber. You probably have guessed: yes, we will again use Agile Travel site in this case study.

Create Selenium-Cucumber Test Project

In TestWise, select menu 'File' → 'New Project' to create a new test project, this time, choose Cucumber as the test framework.

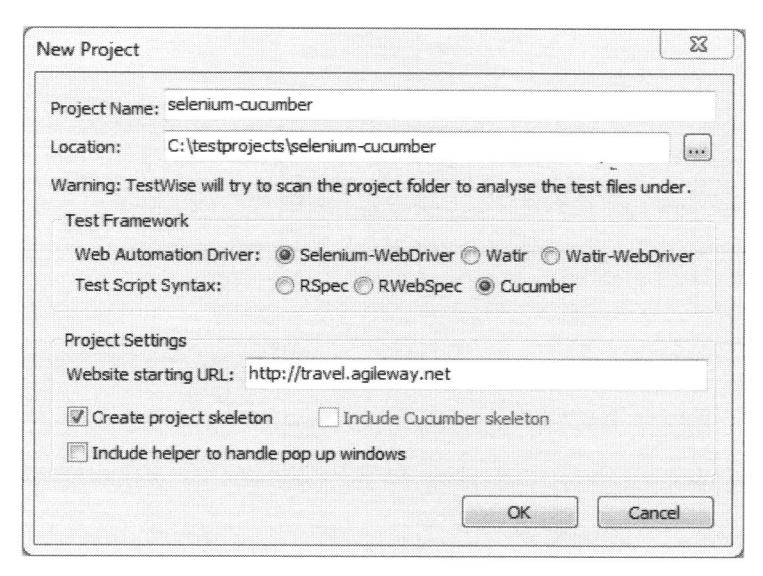

When a Cucumber project is created, we see a slightly more complex project structure than RSpec.

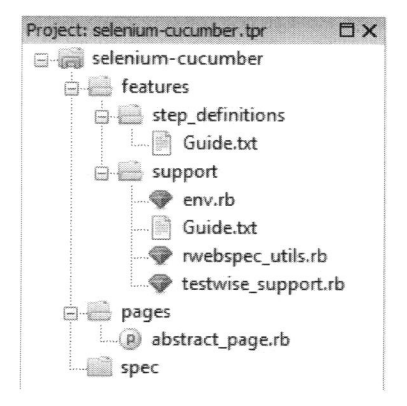

We again see the *pages/* folder, yes, that's for page classes. We are going to reuse all the page classes developed previously. Copy all page classes under *\ch13-selenium\case_study-selenium-rspec\pages* to this *pages* folder.

Raw Selenium-WebDriver in Cucumber

Now we are ready to create a new feature (aka. cucumber test) file for testing user to sign in. Select menu 'File' → 'New File'

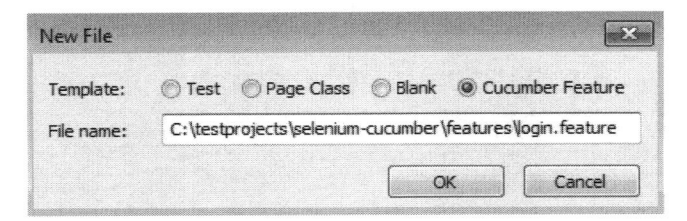

Now a new file *login.feature* is created:

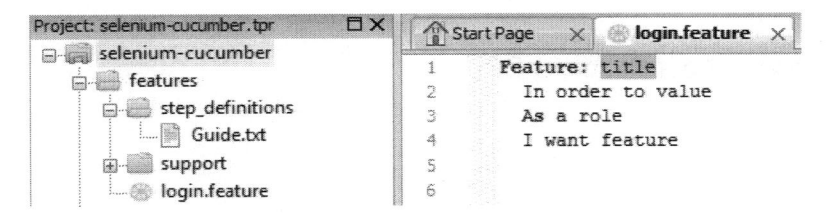

The feature section (as shown above) is pretty much plain text. We now add one test scenario for user to sign in (tip: you can use 'sce' snippet in TestWise to create a scenario):

```
Scenario: Registered user can log in successfully
  Given I am on the home page
  When enter user name "agileway" and password "testwise"
  And click "Sign in" button
  Then I am logged in
```

Once we are happy with steps in the scenario, we need to create step definitions for them. To do that, right click on any of above steps, and select "Create (XXX) feature steps in"

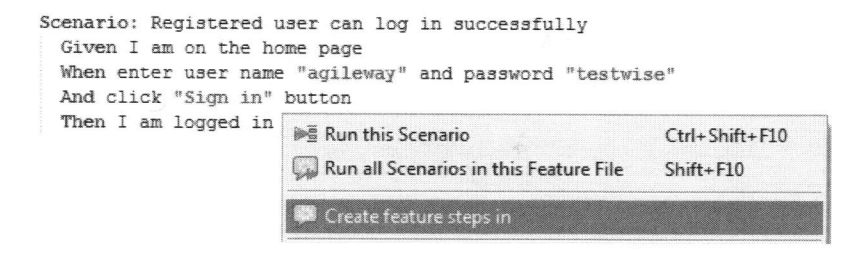

```
Scenario: Registered user can log in successfully
  Given I am on the home page
  When enter user name "agileway" and password "testwise"
  And click "Sign in" button
  Then I am logged in
```

- Run this Scenario — Ctrl+Shift+F10
- Run all Scenarios in this Feature File — Shift+F10
- Create feature steps in

Specify the file name for the step definition:

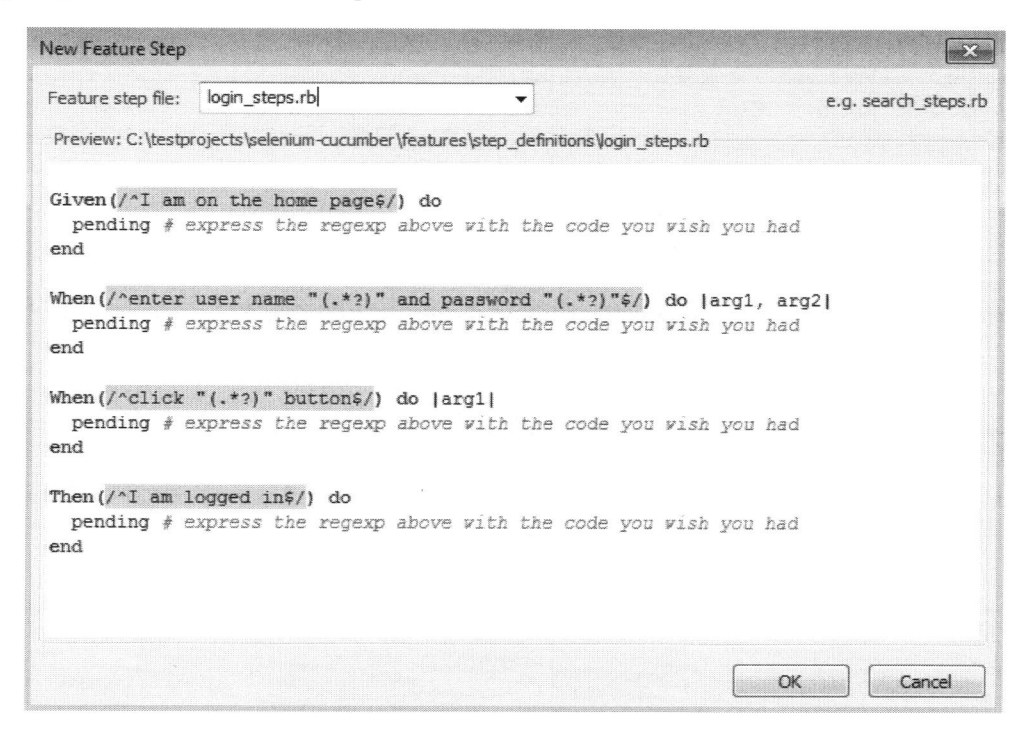

New Feature Step

Feature step file: login_steps.rb   e.g. search_steps.rb

Preview: C:\testprojects\selenium-cucumber\features\step_definitions\login_steps.rb

```ruby
Given(/^I am on the home page$/) do
  pending # express the regexp above with the code you wish you had
end

When(/^enter user name "(.*?)" and password "(.*?)"$/) do |arg1, arg2|
  pending # express the regexp above with the code you wish you had
end

When(/^click "(.*?)" button$/) do |arg1|
  pending # express the regexp above with the code you wish you had
end

Then(/^I am logged in$/) do
  pending # express the regexp above with the code you wish you had
end
```

This will create file *login_steps.rb* under *features\step_definitions*, which contains the below:

```
Given /^I am on the home page$/ do
  pending # express the regexp above with the code you wish you had
end

When /^enter user name "(.*?)" and password "(.*?)"$/ do |arg1, arg2|
  pending # express the regexp above with the code you wish you had
end

When /^click "(.*?)" button$/ do |arg1|
  pending # express the regexp above with the code you wish you had
end

Then /^I am logged in$/ do
  pending # express the regexp above with the code you wish you had
end
```

As you can see, it is only the step skeleton. Then we need to replace 'pending's with actual test steps. Let's do it one by one.

Step 1. Start on the home page

This step, in the context of testing, is to navigate to the home page of the test site. In *features/support/env.rb*, an instance variable *@browser* is defined to represent the driver. Also in *env.rb*, the global variable $BASE_URL is set to our target site: "http://travel.agileway.net". So replace 'pending' line with selenium-webdriver test step, and get:

```
Given /^I am on the home page$/ do
  @browser.navigate.to($BASE_URL)
end
```

Step 2. Operation: enter user name "agileway" and password "testwise"

This step passes two text values that are shown as arguments ("arg1" and "arg2") in the skeleton:

```
When /^enter user name "(.*?)" and password "(.*?)"$/ do |arg1, arg2|
```

We change them to more meaningful names: *user* and *pass*, and fill the selenium-webdriver test steps:

```
When /^enter user name "(.*?)" and password "(.*?)"$/ do |user, pass|
  @browser.find_element(:id, "username").send_keys(user)
  @browser.find_element(:id, "password").send_keys(pass)
end
```

Step 3. Operation: click "Sign in" button

Similar to the previous step, we change 'arg1' to 'button', to refer value of argument in a Ruby string, wrap it with '#{button}'.

```
When /^click "(.*?)" button$/ do |button|
  @browser.find_element(:xpath,"//input[@value=\"#{button}\"]").click
end
```

Step 4. Assertion: Then I am logged in

The assertion here is a standard Selenium-WebDriver text assertion.

```
Then /^I am logged in$/ do
  expect(@browser.page_source).to include("Welcome agileway")
end
```

Run the test in the same way as for RSpec. Right click the scenario step, and select 'Run this scenario'

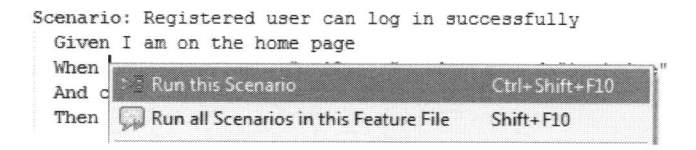

```
Scenario: Registered user can log in successfully
  Given I am on the home page
  When
  And          Run this Scenario              Ctrl+Shift+F10
  Then         Run all Scenarios in this Feature File   Shift+F10
```

A browser (depends on selection of browser type in TestWise) will start up to run the test, and it shall pass.

Use functions and page objects in Cucumber

Here is another cucumber test: selecting oneway trip flight

```
Scenario: Oneway Trip
  Given I am signed in as "agileway"
  When select oneway trip
  And select depart from "Sydney" to "New York" on "07" of "May 2012"
  And click "Continue"
  Then I should see "2012-05-07", "New York" and "Sydney" on next page
```

The step definition for 'Given I am signed in as "agileway"' is

```
Given /^I am signed in as "(.*?)"$/ do |user|
  @browser.find_element(:id, "username").send_keys(user)
  @browser.find_element(:id, "password").send_keys("test")
  @browser.find_element(:xpath,"//input[@value=\"Sign in\"]").click
end
```

You can apply refactorings to cucumber step definitions just like you do to RSpec test scripts. For this step definition, we can see these 3 test steps can be extracted into a reusable function: *sign_in*.

Refactoring: Extract Function

In TestWise, highlight these 3 test steps, select menu 'Refactor' → 'Extract to Function'

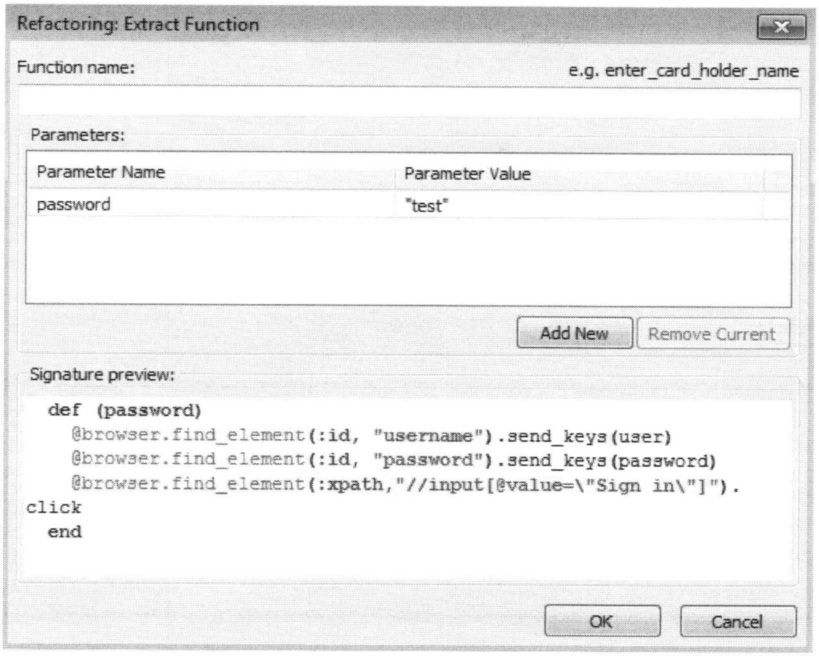

Delete the pre-populated parameter 'password', and add two parameters below in order:

1. user, user
2. password, "test"

and get parameters as shown in this screenshot:

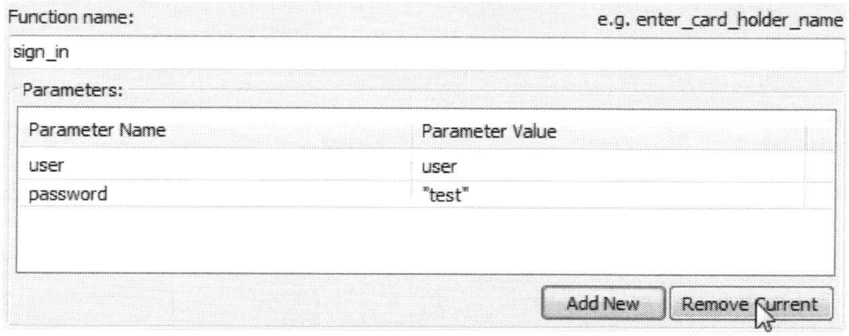

Click 'OK' button to extract out the function. Don't forget to rerun the test after refactoring.

Refactoring: Move to Helper

As TestWise hasn't implemented Move refactoring in cucumber feature steps, we are going to to do this refactoring manually. Select the whole *sign_in* function, cut and paste into the *env.rb* (under features/support). The step definition becomes:

```
Given /^I am signed in as "(.*?)"$/ do |user|
  sign_in("agileway", "testwise")
end
```

Refactoring: Introduce Page Object

Also we realize that after signing in, the user should land on the flight page. We could utilize the page classes (copied over) here. To invoke 'Introduce Page Object' refactoring, type 'ep' followed by the Tab key.

```
Given /^I am signed in as "(.*?)"$/ do |user|
  sign_in("agileway", "testwise")
  expect_page Fl
end           ⓟ FlightPage
```

Select the 'FlightPage', and pre-append '@' in the front of *flight_page*. The complete step definition looks like this:

```
Given /^I am signed in as "(.*?)"$/ do |user|
  sign_in("agileway", "testwise")
  @flight_page = FlightPage.new(@browser)
end
```

In the next step definition (selecting one way trip),

```
When /^select oneway trip$/ do
  pending # express the regexp above with the code you wish you had
end
```

We can simply auto complete the operations defined in *FlightPage* class by typing '@flight_-page.'

```
When /^select oneway trip$/ do
  @flight_page.select_
end                    ⓘ select_arrive_at
                       ⓘ select_depart_from
When /^select          ⓘ select_departure_day
  @flight_pa           ⓘ select_departure_month
end
                       ⓘ select_return_date
When /^click "         ⓘ select_trip_type
  @flight_page
```

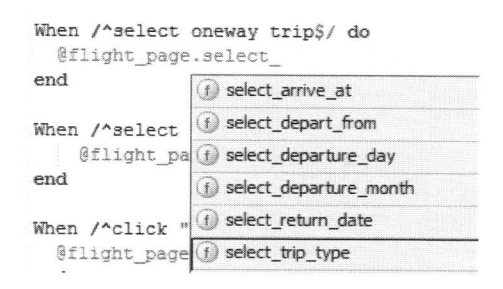

and get

```
When /^select oneway trip$/ do
  @flight_page.select_trip_type("one_way")
end
```

You can see, with the help of page classes (we created in previously), developing cucumber feature steps is easier. I will leave you to implement the remaining tests (scenarios). You can always refer to the example test scripts for this.

Run Cucumber tests from command line

If you have had RubyShell installed, you are ready to execute Cucumber tests. Otherwise, you can install Cucumber with the command below:

```
gem install cucumber
```

To run tests in a feature file:

```
cucumber login.feature
```

To get a HTML test report of executing tests in two cucumber feature files:

```
cucumber -f html login.feature flight_feature > test_report.html
```

To run a specific scenario (test case) in a feature file:

```
cucumber login.feature:15
```

(15 is the line number within the range of the scenario)

Comparison: RSpec and Cucumber

Personally, I like RSpec more for the reasons listed below:

- **Easier to maintain**

  With RSpec tests, there are only two layers: Test Case → Page classes/functions, while Cucumber has three layers: Test Case → Step definitions → Page classes/functions. Extra layers means more difficult to maintain. The steps in Cucumber may look like a sentence in plain English (or your language), a single character change to it needs an update to its step definition.
- **Easier to use execution hooks**

  I like the idea of seeing execution hooks, e.g. before(:each), in the actual test cases, like in RSpec. I am not feeling positive with using Ruby *at_exit* hook in Cucumber for the after(:all) hook.
- **Better tool support** (for now)

  There are more tools supporting RSpec as it has been around longer than Cucumber.

Cucumber tests offer unquestionably superior readability over RSpec. It can be quite useful when customers and business analysts get involved in reading/executing the tests. Having said that, I have worked with customers who are comfortable with RSpec tests as well. Back to the reality, as long as you can maintain, either RSpec or Cucumber is a good solution.

RSpec and Cucumber Co-exists

If you are undecided on RSpec or Cucumber, you can actually organize a test project to support both Behaviour Drive Development frameworks. In TestWise, on creating a new project, select main framework 'RSpec', then click the checkbox "Include Cucumber Skeleton":

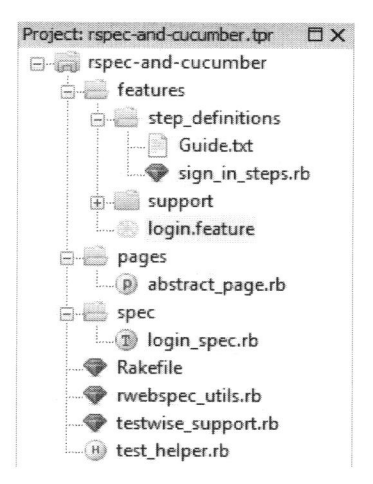

In the project directory, you can create or run RSpec tests or Cucumber tests as you normally do.

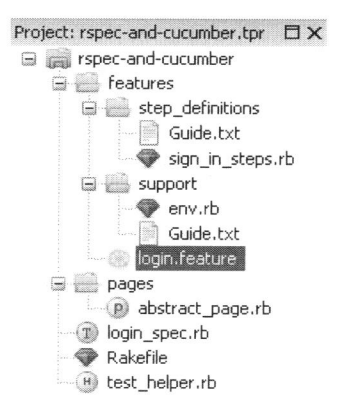

To make things even better, the page objects created are fully reusable between RSpec and Cucumber tests. How good is that!

15. Adopting Test Automation

Congratulations on making it this far. I assume you have developed quite a number of working test scripts of your own and are motivated to start or refine the automated testing process in your project. Here comes the question: where shall I start?

Seek Executive Sponsorship

Without executive support, test automation is difficult to implement well. Let's look at a good example of executive sponsorship on test automation: Google CEO Larry Page receives daily email notification of Android build [NEWS 11c]. It is not hard to imagine that a lot of automated testing happens for each build. Without the assurance of automated testing, you would go crazy if you were to send a "build successful" email to the CEO for code that just compiled OK. So, if Google's CEO sees it was that important, shouldn't your organization or manager too?

If you haven't worked on projects which have done serious test automation, let me tell you, the impact (good of course) that it brings to the project's development process will probably exceed your expectations. Not everyone is comfortable with the changes, at least initially. For example, a programmer used to say "it will be fixed in the stablizing phase where bug convergence ...' when responding to bug reports. Now he works in a project with a solid continuous integration process with automated testing. Someone has to tell him that "Stop what you are doing, the build is broken, fix the defect now." It is a mindset change that is required.

Some people resist changes strongly. When that happens, especially when office politics get in the way, gaining support from senior management is probably the most effective solution. To convince managers to support test automation, you can try from two angles: benefit realization (or damage prevention) and software maintenance.

Benefit Realization

In 2010, my local state's health department upgraded their health payroll system, which failed miserably and caused grief to thousands of health workers. 15 months later, this news headline said it all : "Health payroll will cost up to $220 million to fix, acting director-general admits" [NEWS 11b]. The main reason for this software failure, not surprisingly, according to state's Auditor-General report, is "Pay system not properly tested" [NEWS 10a].

For such a high profile failed software project, 15 months should be plenty time to fix it. However, this is not this case. If you ask me, this is an example of "fix one break three syndrome", that is, developers rush to fix defects under pressure, while one is fixed but break other parts of system (you get the picture).

Some project managers don't pay serious attention to software testing until reaching the user acceptance testing phase. We, including managers themselves, know this is wrong. It is a bit like programmers, few will deny the benefits of Test Driven Development, but how many programmers you have met that actually wrote unit tests before code? The real reason, I think, is that they have never experienced the actual benefits of automated testing which extend far beyond verification.

Software Maintenance

Software support and maintenance are difficult without comprehensive regression test suites. Here are the facts:

- Maintenance programmers have less knowledge about system and are less familiar with the code, at least initially
- Production data is already in place, i.e. any updates need to be very carefully applied
- Business analysts and customers are not readily available

Automated regression tests provide the best safety net. Software maintainers can prevent invalid or corruptive changes to production by running automated regression tests in a controlled environment first. Also team members (including customers) can get to know the application and business logic quickly by running tests. You probably heard this before: automated UI tests are living documentation.

Here is a hard question for managers who don't understand the importance of regression testing: "How can we guarantee that further updates by maintenance programmers won't break current business functions?" Here is my tip though - choose the right time to ask this question :-).

Choose Test Framework

This can be a highly subjective topic, here are some objective factors to consider:

- Simple, concise and easy to read
- Easy to learn and use
- Easy to maintain
- Affordable, so you can get each of your team member a copy
- Freedom, no vendor locking

In "Agile Testing" book, Lisa Crispin and Janet Gregory listed a number of successful projects on automated testing. The top two most used test frameworks are Watir and Selenium. I certainly agree with them. Both Watir and Selenium are free and open-source, and have been around for several years with a big user community behind them.

Watir only supports Internet Explorer. If your application is required to be tested on Firefox, or even Chrome apart from Internet Explorer, Selenium is the one to go with.

For some frameworks, you have options to choose which language binding to use. For example, Selenium tests can be written in multiple programming languages such as Java, C# and Ruby. Quite commonly, I heard the saying such as "This is a Java project, so we shall write tests in Java as well". I disagree. Software testing is to verify whether programmer's work meets customer's needs. In a sense, testers are representing customers. Testers should have more weight on deciding the test syntax than programmers. Plus why would you mandate that your testers have to have the same programming language skills as the programmers. In my subjective view, scripting languages such as Ruby and Python are more suitable for test scripts than compiled languages such as C and Java (Confession: I have been programming in Java for over 10 years). By the way, we call them test **scripts**, for a reason.

Regardless of which framework is selected, it is a good idea to allocate some time for the team to run a trail. A logical way is to try one typical project with two or three candidates. Write dozens of real tests and see how easy for testers to learn and how they cope with application changes.

> **Thoughts on free and open-source test frameworks**
>
> According to Richard Stallman, the founder of the Free Software Foundation, "Free software is software is a matter of liberty, not price", as in 'free speech', not as in 'free beer'" [FSF]. Some organisations reject free software without understanding the real meaning of 'free'. In terms of support, personally I don't remember experiencing good support from large software organisations. Many probably agree with me that Google is the best resource to get help nowadays. For organisations who really want assurance, there are companies and test automation coaches providing professional services on open-source tools.
>
> In 'Armageddon', an american disaster film, the human race faces extinction, NASA launches two space shuttles to save the earth. These two space shuttles named *Freedom* and *Independence*. It surprises me that when software projects come to choosing the testing framework/tool, highly priced proprietary commercial ones often win (here I remind you of Michael Feather's 'Test Automation Tools are Snake Oil' article), freedom and independence seem to be at the bottom of list for consideration.

Select Test Tool

Once the test framework is chosen, the next step is tool selection. With free and open-source frameworks such as Watir or Selenium, you can create test scripts with NotePad and run them from command line, though it won't be very productive after you have a number of test scripts to manage. The use of recorders has always been controversial. My opinion is that recorders can be very helpful if used wisely.

To make automated testing successful, collaboration is essential. Here I mean mainly the collaboration between testers and programmers. To avoid unnecessary confusion, team members shall use the same tool to view, edit and run automated test scripts. I am generally against using the same tool as programmer's IDE, as this inherently put programmers in a dominant position over testers.

Run as part of Build Process

As we all know, test maintenance is the biggest challenge in test automation. The best way to counter-attack is to execute the test scripts as soon as programmers are ready to integrate. In other words, shorten the feedback loops. A simple rule is to try running all tests at least once each day. The best practice is to incorporate functional testing into the continuous build process.

The test results shall be easily accessible to all team members, commonly made available on an internal web site. Therefore, programmers can act quickly whenever test failures occurred. Also it allows the test reports and scripts to state that often hard things to say like : "It's not working."

Find a Mentor

It is not uncommon to hear people have personal trainers (for their physical health). For automated testing (a rare skill set that is rare among project members), it is surprising to know very few projects have actually even thought about seeking professional help on this. Here I am talking about real mentoring service on issues or challenges that the test team faces, not some kind of 3-month test process review, which is often a waste of time and money (or worse, some might even try to get you to buy highly priced tools). As I said before, testing is high on practice and light on theory. An experienced test automation coach can help develop a fair amount of useful test scripts within a day, rather than a useless report.

Just like in the fairy tale 'Princess and the Pea', to tell a real princess can be really simple: using a pea. OK, let me be more specific. Here are some of questions you should ask your test coach candidate:

- Our test execution hangs on an IE security warning pop up, How can I click the OK button in Popup window to let test continue?
- How to click the second link with same text in one page?
- We now have 100 tests run for 1 hour, how can we reduce the feedback loop?

Comparing to other type of consulting in software industry, test coaching is probably the most effective and economical one. An experienced test coach can answer your specific questions within hours, sometimes even in minutes, as they don't need to know your software architecture and just analyse the problem. The knowledge they have gained from other projects can often be directly applied to yours, thus saving you days of non-productive effort (or worse, trying in the dark). Test script files are generally very small, so they can be easily exchanged between the team and the coach, which avoids misunderstandings. Furthermore, if possible, you can even give the test coach the access to your public test site, so that he or she can better help you by being able to run the test scripts.

Manage Expectation

Even if your team are ready to do test automation, don't expect that every one is as enthusiastic and motivated as you.

An architect once told me "I was initially doubtful (on test automation), but after seeing no defects for a couple of months over frequent releases, I am convinced." From my observation, a large percentage of people fall into this category. If you do well with good communication, many of them will be on your side. There are, however, negative people, FUD (Fear, uncertainty and doubt) comes to them when facing changes.

The main challenge resides in getting support from programmers. For example, a tester identifies that the system needs a database reset facility to allow executing automated tests quickly. When the request is sent to developers, the development team leader may simply ignore it as he sees no immediate value (or more likely, doesn't know how). A more common case, testers would like IDs to be added to HTML elements for easier identification, a very simple job for programmers with little effort. But this can be hard to get it done in real life.

Practically, we cannot automate everything. Test frameworks, applications under testing and testers' skills all have certain limitations. So don't get fixated on the idea of 100% full automation, this will only add unnecessary stress. The adoption of test automation is NOT all or nothing. With each test case you develop, you get one extra layer of protection. Do make the effort to keep all the automated tests up to date to keep your protection intact.

Solo Test Automation

You may ask: without team support, can I still do automated testing? My answer is yes. Despite of emergence of acronyms such as TDD, BDD and ATDD in recent years, still, only a small percentage of projects have actually achieved some degree of success with test automation. If your project is not on the list, it is quite normal. Maybe you are the one to make it happen.

You are reading this book because you have the desire for a change. Don't let some short-sight managers kill that. You can still adopt test automation to make your own work as effective (and fun) as possible.

Here are some suggestions for solo test automation specialists:

- Start with easy and tedious test cases, automated them first. This will get you runs on the board.

- Run all tests often, aiming to keep existing tests correct and updated as priority
- Set up a mechanism to trigger test run easily
- Create your own source control for test scripts (if there is no one already)

It shouldn't take long for people to notice your achievements. Some may say *"Great! But how could you find so many defects so quickly? The build was just released this morning"*. Then you show them the automated tests. It is much easier and more powerful to show and demonstrate than explain without something to show.

Common Mistakes

> "A failure is not always a mistake, it may simply be the best one can do under the circumstances. The real mistake is to stop trying." - Burrhus Frederic Skinner, psychologist, author, inventor and social philosopher

Test automation is rarely done successfully, in other words, many mistakes were made. I hope this book, particularly Appendix II, will give the confidence. We all learn from mistakes, let's examine some common mistakes in test automation attempts.

Aiming too long

> "Aim too long and you won't get to fire." - John Grinnell, Author and Leadership & Organizational Development Consultant

This is typically found in some medium and large organisations. A group of architects, test manager, senior testers and the program director form a special group to work on test automation strategy. Several months later (with countless meetings and reports), this group quietly wound up. It seems that nothing was ever happened.

The reason is simple, test automation is so practical that its knowledge can only be gained by doing it. The chances are that no one in the group has ever written more than 10 automated tests. How could they come out a good test automation strategy?

Some may ask what my test automation strategy is. I do have a test strategy, it is all in the test scripts. Automated test scripts, honestly, I think, has the 'magical power' to guide you (think about 'Test Driven Development') if you care to listen.

Problem	Area to check
hard to develop and read	test framework
not supporting Chrome?	test framework
difficult to maintain	test design
not efficient, takes long to develop or debug	testing tool
even one test execution takes long time	did your team implement 'reset database'
not working well among the team	test script convention, testing tool
feedback too long	CI Process

My advice: Task planning for the first 5 days in test automation trial

- Day 1: write 2 real tests at minimum
- Day 2: write 3 more and maintain 2 existing tests
- Day 3: write 5 more and maintain 5 existing tests
- Day 4: write 10 more and maintain 10 existing tests
- Day 5: write 10 more tests and run all tests (30) in a CI server

Juggling with test frameworks

This is an example of 'aiming too long'. Because this mistake is too typical, I single it out. I often get the following comments from our customers:

- What do you think of watir-webdriver?
- Which syntax framework shall I use: RSpec or Cucumber?
- Can I use Capybara in TestWise?

Some of these questions are from the same person. I couldn't help thinking he must have been keeping trying something new. When I asked him how many tests he had written, there was no reply.

While being open-minded to new technologies is good, the fundamentals of test automation won't change much. For example, 'Page objects' pattern has been around for decades and it is still one of the best test design principals. In terms of frameworks, I used many of them. The key to successful test automation is not how many frameworks you know. It is how many maintainable tests you can write and execute them efficiently with prompt feedback.

There are many kind of these "automated testers". They have an amazing ability to get away from writing actual tests, but constantly talking about test automation. What a pity, doing test automation is so much fun.

> ### Be aware of testing strategies from new team members
>
> I met a few (our customers mentioned some too) such programmers or testers. Right after they joined the team, maybe for the purpose of raising his/her status, they started to point out the development process was no good or the current testing process is flawed. Test Automation is an easy area to be picked on, for the following reasons:
>
> - not many people know or understand test automation
> - easily demonstrable (download a trial testing tool, record and play an automated test)
>
> However, the difficulties of test automation lie in test maintenance. If the team believed in him, asked him to look after the test automation. Weeks later, nothing really happened except excuses.
>
> Nowadays, with the influence of agile development, some programmers pretend to know test automation even if they have done barely more than HelloWorld tests. Their logic *"If I can program, I surely can write automated tests"* is very wrong. It is not just my view, check out this interview "Testing the Limits with Google's Patrick Copeland"[a].
>
> On the other hand, if you are really lucky, the new member could be the one you have been waiting for, and that he can really do test automation. He would write tests on the first day and would be able to write more while maintaining the existing ones.
>
> ---
> [a] http://blog.utest.com/testing-the-limits-with-patrick-copeland-part-ii/2010/02/

Overestimate test automation effort

For large organisations, especially government departments, some middle level managers and software architects learned that the best way to keep the job - that is to the problem bigger by having lots of meetings and defining all kinds of processes. The end result seems not that important, that's why many organizations have more than one round of failed test automation attempts. Previous failures add more reasons to be more cautious, therefore, more meetings and more processes.

Why management is so cautious about adopting test automation puzzles me. Different from deployment architecture (e.g. Windows to Linux, SQL Server to MySQL) and software architecture changes (.NET to Java), the introduction of test automation has

- No impact to customers
- No risks
- No immediate dependent software impact
- Low cost (unless wanting to waste a lot money)

Why not just simply do it? Writing test scripts against your applications, and see whether the approach fits.

The 'low cost' is quite clear now as the open-source Selenium leads every testing tool or framework (in terms of testing job ads) and is widely used by big organisations such as Google and FaceBook. However, some managers still favour ultra expensive and vendor-locking commercial testing tools, which is beyond my comprehension.

Underestimate test automation effort

It is easy to under-estimate the test automation effort too. For a long time, test automation was sold as snake oil by large companies for their own financial gains. After seeing so many costly failures, few software managers would believe that test automation is easy as advertised by the vendor's salesman. However, some are still willing to believe that developing automated test scripts is as simple as 'record and playback', and the word 'auto' was misinterpreted as: after the initial effort, then all will run well thereafter.

This is more common in small start ups. The business owner's main focus is the first release (and release milestones thereafter). For them, software features mean money. They tend to ignore the accumulating technique debt which slows down or even halt the software development. Manual testing obviously has its limits. They look for a quick test automation solution to quickly get over the current 'bugs everywhere' situation.

> ### Few TestWise customers take up free complimentary test automaton coaching service
>
> Our company AgileWay offers commercial test automation coaching service. We understand some programmers/testers are willing to learn, but might find hard to get the manger's approval to purchase dedicated test automation mentoring. We offer a complimentary support to TestWise Pro customers, if they could replicate the issue in a test against our sample web application, we will provide the help for free.
>
> However, while we often receive requests for help with test scripts, which we were unable to fulfil for two reasons: the target applications are usually not accessible for us and it would be unfair for customers who purchased the coaching service. What surprised us

> was that few has taken the complimentary coaching service. This shows that they wanted the help on test automation, but they were not willing to spend money (for mentoring) or time to replicate the issue against our sample application. It seems many of them were not keen enough to put in extra effort to seek the solution. I just hope that they won't give up the test automation so easily.

Managers/Developers think "maintaining automated tests slows down the development"

This might sound absurd (blunt statements like this might get sacked on the spot at Google or Facebook). But this actually happens quite often. The real reasons are:

- Developers or tester are not willing to learn
- Software architecture was wrong
- The automated tests are not written properly

If you sense FUD (Fear, Uncertainty and Doubt) in your team members, it is a management issue.

Well designed software is easier to automated test. It might be true that the software design was not optimal or lack of support for test automation. Review your software design. For example, does your application support database reset?

Writing maintainable automated tests requires knowledge and practice. Study this book well and follow the good sample tests (check out the Resources section). The most time-saving (and cost effective) way is to get a test automation coach.

No Test Automation Mentors

If your children want to learn to play tennis, you will find a coach for them. The simple fact is that, if you don't possess the skill, seeking help from others is probably the most cost effective way. However, software managers usually don't think this way on test automation.

Project management rather fail the test automation effort than seek the help from test automation coaches for the reasons below:

- **"It is a secret trial"**. The root cause is that the teams have very low confidence from the start, so they want to keep it quiet.
- **"Fear of losing reputation"**. Testing are regarded as lower level (I believe the examples of focusing on testing by LinkedIn and Facebook will eventually will change that view). Big organizations might think seeking external help on testing is not necessary. Furthermore, the one developer/tester who leads the test automation trial is usually regarded as the senior authority in the area within the company. It is easier to blame the tool or framework, rather than admit lack of knowledge.
- **"Not ready to change"**. An experienced senior software manager shall know the impact (good, of course) of automated testing will bring to the organization. The fundamental changes of the testing approach inevitably will affect many existing procedures and might upset some people, giving up is the easiest thing to do.
- **"Too expensive, cannot find good ones"**. The word 'coaching' or 'mentoring' is often associated with 'expensive'. This is not necessarily true, especially for real test automation coaches.

"One day test coaching changed my life"

I once was asked to provide test coaching service to a government project, the project director has already allocated initial 5-day consulting budget.

On the first day, after brief introduction (personnel, testing process and the application), I said to the manager, I would like to work with your tester to write some test scripts together. Kate, the tester to work with me, was new to the test automation. She had some programming experience before but not in Ruby.

Kate was so keen on test automation that, prior to my coming, she has read my book (the one you are reading now) and done all the exercises. Furthermore, she had started writing test scripts for the applications and noted down the issues she was having. Not surprisingly, she learned very well. At the end of the day, we have done quite a lot test scripts, real test cases against the real application.

Maybe the outcome far exceeded the manager's expectation (seeing many automated tests running), he concluded that further consulting was no long required. It's fine for me, but pity the continuous integration was not set up to run tests through. Anyway, months later, I met Kate at the train station, she was happy with the job (the title changed to "Senior technical test lead"). She said to me : "that one day coaching changed my life".

Lack of Continuous Integration Process

Continuous Integration has been talked a lot, but rarely done. Try to answer the questions below:

1. How many projects you worked have a constantly running CI server?
2. If so, does it include running unit testing (I mean whole unit test suite)?
3. Does it deploy the project artifacts (e.g. war files) to server(s) as a part of CI build?
4. Does it run automated UI tests?
5. Does it distribute automated UI tests to multiple build machines to execute in parallel?

The simple fact is that test automation cannot be successful without a good CI process.

Wrap up

I have seen and heard many so called 'agile projects' without automated functional UI tests at all. I was quite surprised at first, but not any more. Yes, test automation may be unknown to you or you have heard some projects not doing it well. I hope this book can give you a boost of some encouragement. Just like an old saying, "If you never never do, you never never know".

Happy **Fun**ctional Testing!

Appendix 1 Functional Test Refactoring Catalog

This is a list of functional test refactorings that are in the same format as the original 'Refactoring' book.

- Move Test Steps
- Extract to Function
- Move Function to Helper
- Extract to Page Class
- Introduce Page Object
- Rename

Move Test Scripts

You have same set beginning or ending test steps in multiple test cases

Move common test steps into shared sections that run before or after each test case

Benefits

- Concise and Focused tests
- Reduce Duplication, DRY

Motivation

Long and similar test cases are harder to maintain. By grouping test cases and utilize shared sections, it is possible to make tests cases concise and more distinguishable.

Prerequisite

- Multiple (grouped) test cases are allowed in a single test script file
- Shared sections (execution hooks) where the test steps are executed before or after each testest case

Mechanics

- Identify same test steps that are common to each test case
- Select the test steps in one test case
- Move them to corresponding sections that run before or after each test case
- Delete repeated test steps in remaining test cases
- Run all the test cases that has changed

Example

'Move Refactoring' is supported in TestWise.

Assume we have two test cases in a test script file: user_spec.rb (in RWebSpec)

```ruby
before(:all) do
  open_browser("http://mycoolsite.com")
end

story "User can update profile" do
  login_as("bob", "test")
  click_link("Profile")
  click_link("Update profile")
  enter_text("postcode", "37201")
  click_button("Update")
  expect(page_text).to include("PostCode: 37201")
  click_button("Logout")
end

story "User can change password" do
  login_as("bob", "test")
  click_link("Profile")
  click_link("Change password")
  enter_text("current_pass", "test")
  enter_text("new_pass", "new")
  enter_text("new_pass_confirm", "new")
  click_button("Change")
  click_button("Logout")
  login_as("bob", "new")
```

```
    click_button("Logout")
  end
```

We identified first two test steps between the two test cases are the same:

```
login_as("bob", "test")
click_link("Profile")
```

and two tests share the same ending test step as well:

```
click_button("Logout")
```

Both can be moved to the execution hooks. We first start moving the two beginning steps (to before each test case) by highlighting it.

```
story "User can update profile" do
  sign_in("bob", "test")
  click_link("Profile")
    click_link("Update profile")
```

Select menu 'Refactor' → 'Move', or press 'Alt+F7' in TestWise.

Refactor	Run Tools Window Help	
	Rename ...	Shift+F6
	Copy...	Shift+F5
	Move...	Shift+F7
	Move Function to Helper	Ctrl+Alt+H
	Extract to Function...	Ctrl+Alt+M
	Extract to Page Function...	Ctrl+Alt+G
	Introduce Page Object...	Ctrl+Alt+V

Select target section 'before(:each)'

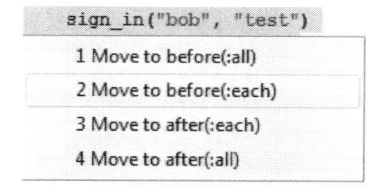

```
sign_in("bob", "test")
```
1 Move to before(:all)
2 Move to before(:each)
3 Move to after(:each)
4 Move to after(:all)

Preview the changes, (tick the checkbox to apply the same refactoring to other detected test cases)

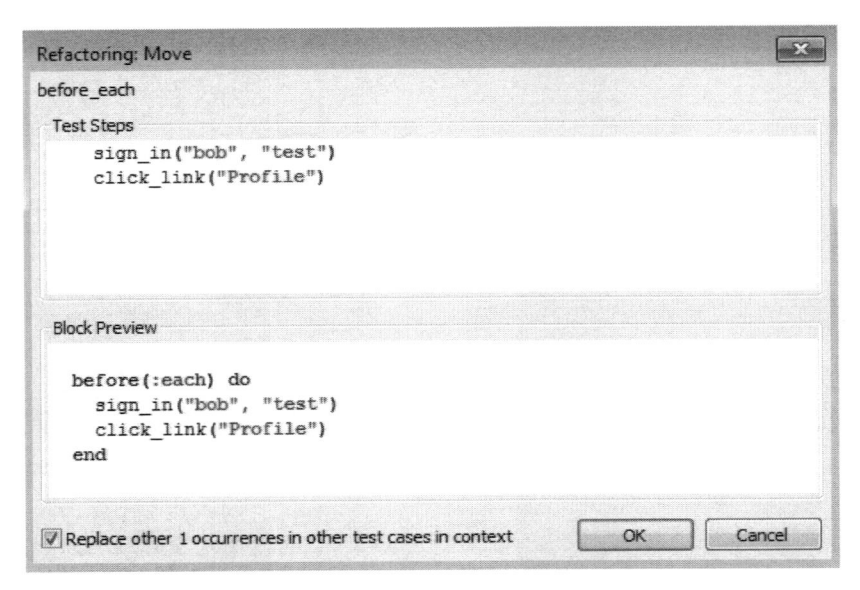

```
Refactoring: Move
before_each
  Test Steps
      sign_in("bob", "test")
      click_link("Profile")

  Block Preview
      before(:each) do
        sign_in("bob", "test")
        click_link("Profile")
      end

  ☑ Replace other 1 occurrences in other test cases in context      [ OK ]   [ Cancel ]
```

Then we get

```
before(:each) do
  login_as("bob", "test")
  click_link("Profile")
end

story "User can update profile" do
  click_link("Update profile")
  #...
end

story "User can change password" do
  click_link("Change password")
  #...
end
```

Please note that those test steps in second test case were also removed.

Run the test cases to make sure it is still running OK.

Re-applying the same process to move the test step happens at end of each test case.

```
click_button("Logout")
```

This time select 'Move to after(:each)' refactoring, then get final version below:

```ruby
require 'rwebspec'

describe "User Profile" do
  include TestHelper

  before(:all) do
    open_browser("http://mycoolsite.com")
  end

  before(:each) do
    login_as("bob", "test")
    click_link("Profile")
  end

  after(:each) do
    click_button("Logout")
  end

  story "User can update profile" do
    click_link("Update profile")
    enter_text("postcode", "37201")
    click_button("Update")
    expect(page_text).to contain("PostCode: 37201")
  end

  story "User can change password" do
    click_link("Change password")
    enter_text("current_pass", "test")
    enter_text("new_pass", "new")
    enter_text("new_pass_confirm", "new")
```

```
    click_button("Change")
    click_button("Logout")
    login_as("bob", "new")
  end

end
```

Apart from moving selected test steps to before or after each test case, you may also move the test steps to sections where it can be executed before or after all the test cases: `before(:all)` and `after(:all)`.

Extract Function

You have long logically grouped test steps performing a common operation

Extract them into a reusable function

Benefits

- Concise and Reusable
- Reduce Duplication, DRY

Motivation

For well understood operations such as user login and credit card payment (formed with a set of individual test steps), it is better to replace them with a reusable function.

Prerequisite

- N/A

Mechanics

- Identify test steps that are common and reusable
- Select the test steps
- Extract them into a function, give a meaningful name
- Replace original steps with a call to the function
- Run all the test cases that has changed

Example

'Extract to Function' is supported in TestWise.

Assume we have a test script file with two cases on testing online payments.

```
story "Purchase one item, pay by Master card" do
   select one product
   add to shopping cart
  click_button("Check out")

  select_option("card_type", "Master Card")
  enter_text("name", "John Smith")
  enter_text("card_number", "5242424242424242")
  click_button("Pay now")

  receipt_page = expect_page ReceiptPage
end

story "Purchase multiple items with quantities, Visa" do
   select one product
   select another product twice
   add to shopping cart
  click_button("Check out")

  select_option("card_type", "Visa")
  enter_text("name", "John Smith")
  enter_text("card_number", "4242424242424242")
  click_button("Pay now")

  receipt_page = expect_page ReceiptPage
end
```

We identified the following test steps that fills in the credit card details - a common and possible reusable function:

```
select_option("credit_card", "Master Card")
enter_text("name", "John Smith")
enter_text("card_number", "5242424242424242")
click_button("Pay now")
```

Highlight them and select the menu 'Refactor' → 'Extract Function', or press 'Ctrl+Alt+M' in TestWise.

Menu Extract Function

Preview the changes and enter a function name, in this case, 'pay_by_credit_card'

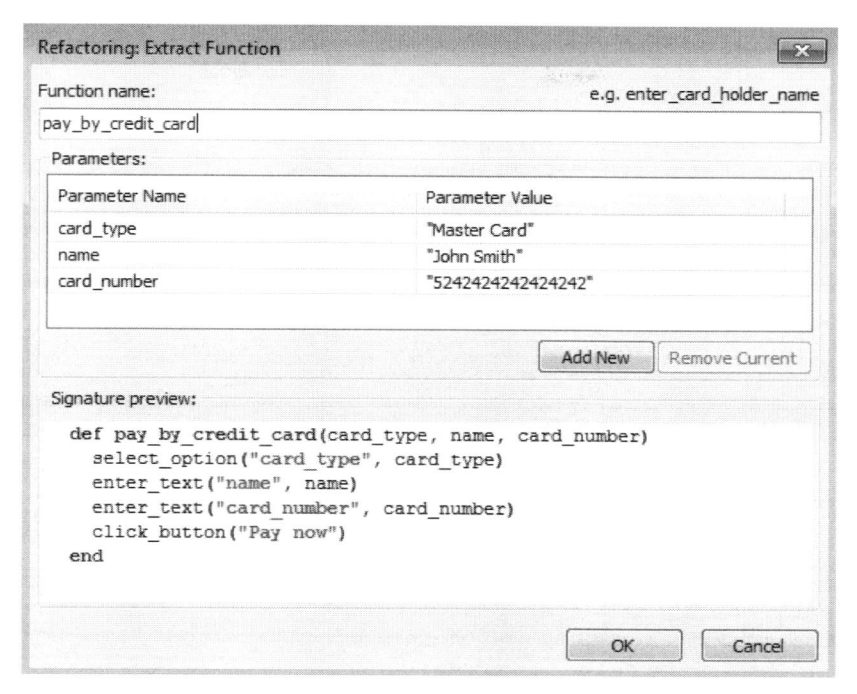

Extract Function Preview

we get

```
def pay_by_credit_card(card_type, name, card_number)
  select_option("card_type", card_type)
  enter_text("name", name)
  enter_text("card_number", card_number)
  click_button("Pay now")
end

story "Purchase one item, pay by Master card" do
  # select one product
  # add to shopping cart
  click_button("Check out")
  pay_by_credit_card("Master Card", "John Smith", "5242424242424242")
  receipt_page = expect_page ReceiptPage
end
```

The "*(card_type, name, card_number)*" after function name '*pay_by_credit_card*' are called parameters, which are used to supply different value to the function. We will now use this newly created *pay_by_credit_card function* in next test case.

```
story "Purchase multiple items with quantities, Visa" do
  # select one product
  # select another product twice
  # add to shopping cart
  click_button("Check out")
  pay_by_credit_card("Visa", "John Citizen", "4242424242424242")
  receipt_page = expect_page ReceiptPage
end
```

Move Function to Helper

You have use the same functions defined in separate test scripts files

Move the function to the shared helper

Benefits

- Reusable
- Auto-complete-able

Motivation

As a common practice, all test scripts in a project shares a common helper. By moving a function to the helper, it is made available to all test cases.

Prerequisite

- N/A

Mechanics

- Identify a function
- Move to the helper
- Rerun tests

Example

Move the cursor to the function's definition (in the example, *sign_in*), select the menu 'Refactor' → 'Move to Helper' in TestWise.

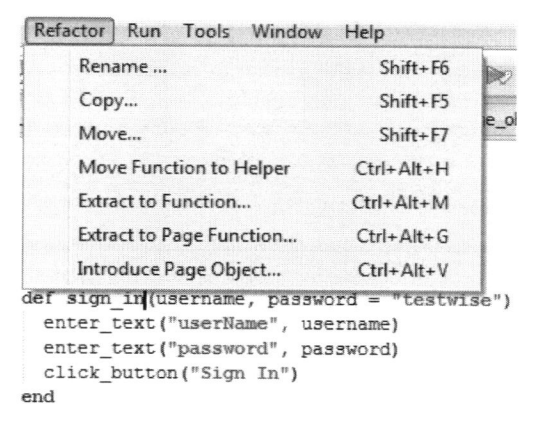

Move to helper menu

This function will be moved to the *test_helper.rb*.

To use this function in another test script, press 'Ctrl+Space', it will show in the auto-complete list.

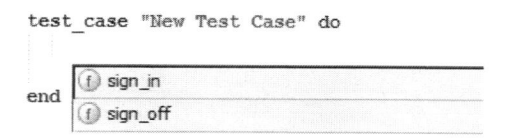

Auto complete function

When selecting the function, the parameters (if any) will appear in the call tip popup.

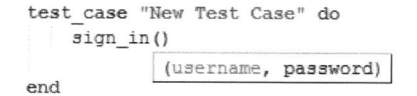

functional call tip

Extract to Page Class

You have long logically grouped test steps

Extract test operations on a web page into a Page Class

Benefits

- DRY
- Concise
- Reusable
- Easy to maintain
- DSL, easy to read
- Auto complete via tool support

Prerequisite

N/A

Motivation

Application changes are usually identified by pages, like "on XXX page, changed Y button to Z". To maintain test scripts in linear test steps form with application changes is hard. By grouping test operations on a web page into an abstract Page Class, if is a lot easier to find test steps affected by application changes and the update only needs to be applied in one place.

Mechanics

- Identify operations on a web page
- Select first operation on page
- Create a Page Class file, giving a meaningful name
- Create a function in the page class with selected operation
- Replace original test step with reference to page class' operation
- Rerun all tests

Example

'Extract Page Class' is supported in TestWise.

Move the cursor to first test operation on a page (in this example, *click_radio_options("tripType", "return")*)

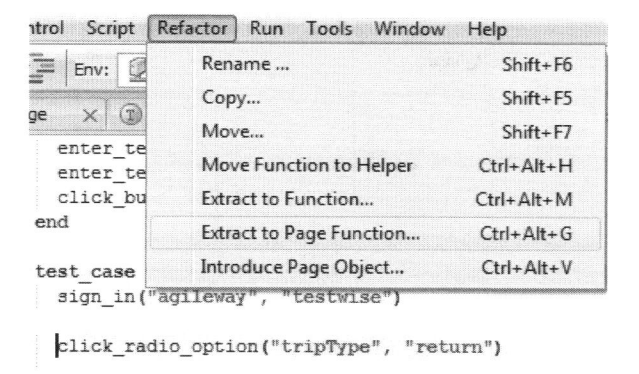

A dialog shows up, enter page name (in CamelCase) and the function name (lowercase connected with underscore) for the operation.

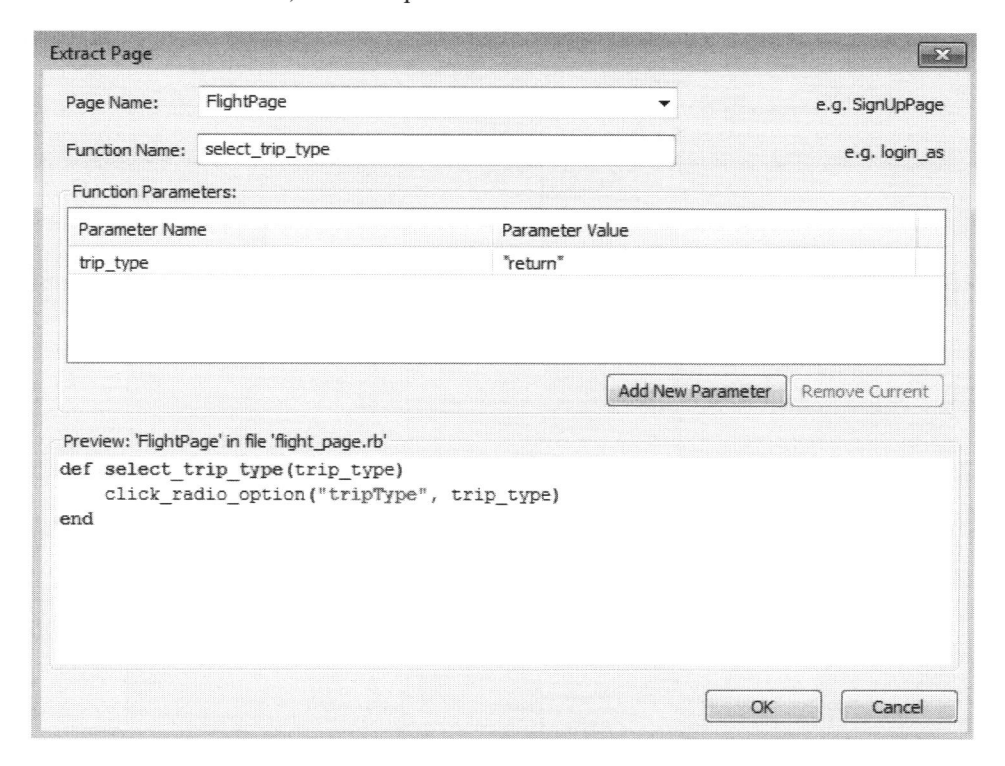

Press OK, a new page file (containing the named page class) is created

220   Appendix 1 Functional Test Refactoring Catalog

```
require File.join(File.dirname(__FILE__), "abstract_page.rb")

class FlightPage < AbstractPage

  def initialize(driver)
    super(driver, "") # <= TEXT UNIQUE TO THIS PAGE
  end

  def select_trip_type(trip_type)
    click_radio_option("tripType", trip_type)
  end

end
```

The (first) test operation is replaced with the page object's function call.

```
test_case "(Refactored version) Book Flight" do
  sign_in("agileway", "testwise")

  flight_page = expect_page FlightPage
  flight_page.select_trip_type("return")

  select_option("fromPort", "New York")
```

Continue extracting the remaining operations on the page in the same way, and operations will be added the page class.

Rerun the tests.

Introduce Page Object

Want to use a defined Page Class

Introduce a page object

Benefits

- Consistent naming
- Auto complete via tool support

Motivation

Knowing the page class for the page has been created, want to reuse it.

Prerequisite

- Page classes defined

Mechanics

- Show up a list of defined page classes
- Select target page class
- A page object of selected page class is defined

Example

'Introduce Page Object' is supported in TestWise.

Enter 'ep' then press 'Tab' key in TestWise, all defined page class names will show up for selection.

```
story "New Test Case" do
    expect_page |
                    (P) AbstractPage
    end
                    (P) FlightPage
```

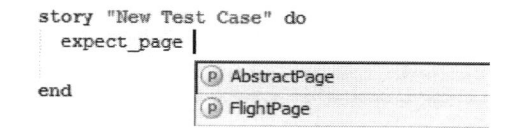

Select a page class, navigate to the menu 'Refactor' → 'Introduce Page Object'

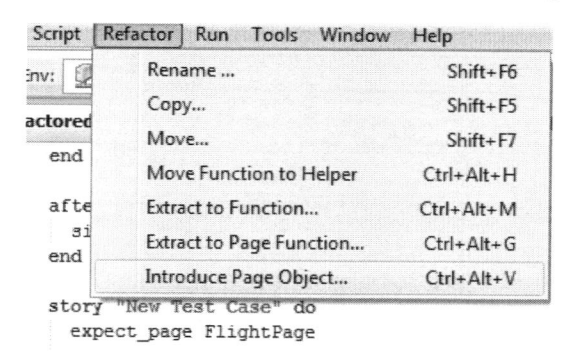

```
Script  Refactor  Run  Tools  Window  Help
inv:        Rename ...                Shift+F6
            Copy...                   Shift+F5
actored
            Move...                   Shift+F7
    end
            Move Function to Helper   Ctrl+Alt+H
    afte    Extract to Function...    Ctrl+Alt+M
      si
    end     Extract to Page Function... Ctrl+Alt+G
            Introduce Page Object...  Ctrl+Alt+V
story "New Test Case" do
    expect_page FlightPage
```

A page object (*flight_finder_page*) is created.

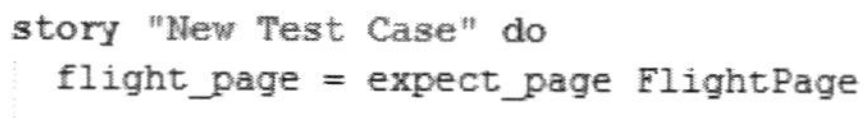

```
story "New Test Case" do
    flight_page = expect_page FlightPage
```

To call a function defined in the Page Class, type '.' after the page object, all function names in the page class will show up for selection.

```
story "New Test Case" do
  flight_page = expect_page FlightPage
  flight_page.
end                    click_continue
                       select_departure_day
```

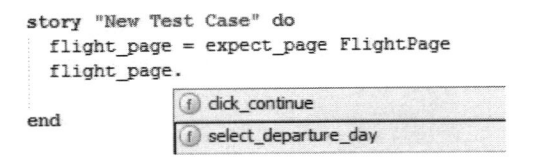

Rename

The name of a function does not reveal its purpose

Change function name

Benefits

- keep test scripts readability

Motivation

Incorrect names and terminology can cause confusion. This applies to test scripts, especially in projects whose customers are involved with testing. More importantly, consistent naming makes test maintenance easier.

Prerequisite

- N/A

Mechanics

- Go to a function declaration or a reference to a function
- Find all references of selected function
- Replace function name in declaration and all references with new name
- Rerun all tests

Example

'Rename' refactoring is supported in TestWise.

On the event registration page, the term '*surname*' has been change to '*last_name*',

Find a reference of surname test step in the test case - '*event_registration_page.enter_member_surname*', move the cursor to the function's name and navigate to the menu 'Refactor' → 'Rename'.

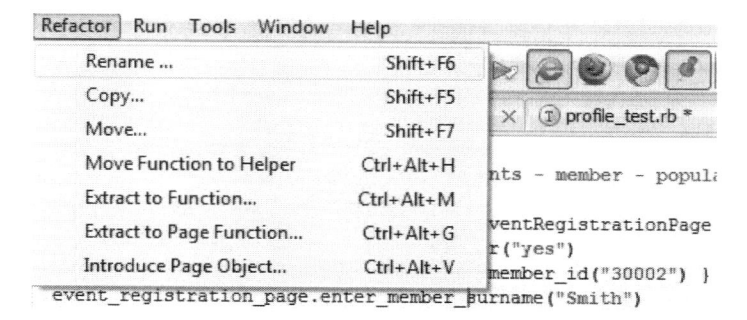

A popup dialog to let you enter new function name

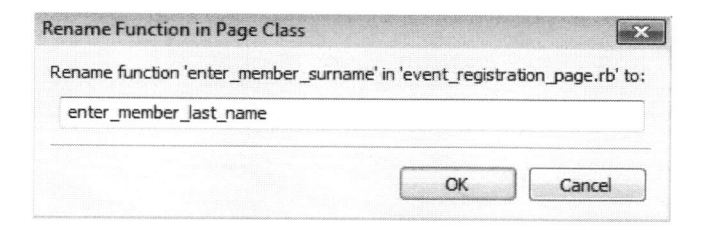

Press 'OK', all references of '*enter_member_surname*' will appear in 'Refactoring Preview', press 'Do Refactor'.

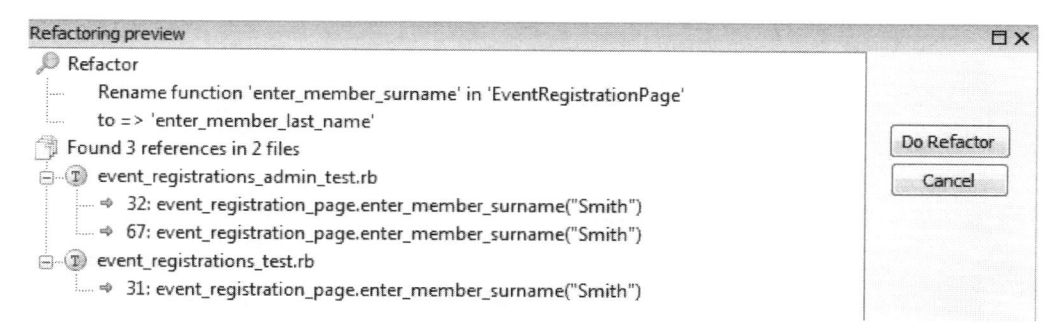

The function declaration in *EventRegistrationPage* and its references are updated with the new name.

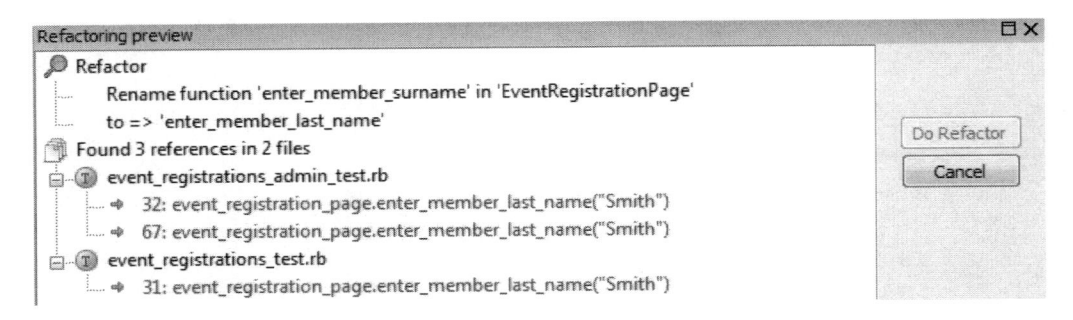

```
Refactoring preview                                          □ ×
 🔍 Refactor
      Rename function 'enter_member_surname' in 'EventRegistrationPage'
      to => 'enter_member_last_name'                    ┌─────────────┐
 📄 Found 3 references in 2 files                        │ Do Refactor │
   └─ ⓣ event_registrations_admin_test.rb              └─────────────┘
        → 32: event_registration_page.enter_member_last_name("Smith")
        → 67: event_registration_page.enter_member_last_name("Smith") │ Cancel │
   └─ ⓣ event_registrations_test.rb
        → 31: event_registration_page.enter_member_last_name("Smith")
```

There are other kinds of rename refactorings as well, such as rename local variable, instance variable and global variable, which are not covered here.

Appendix 2 Test Automation in ClinicWise project

It started about one year ago. One of my relatives was going to open a dental clinic. He mentioned to me that the clinic management software on market were expensive, unintuitive to use and unhelpful support. After a few drinks, I offered to write one for him in my spare time.

I admit it was a bold promise, and I wouldn't do it again. I knew my programming productivity has greatly increased by practicing test automation and CI (have been doing a couple of side projects and one web application for a charity organization). Still, developing this client-waiting application in my spare time was a big challenge.

A few weeks later, the product (I named it ClinicWise[1]) was released into production. The client was quite happy. ClinicWise development is quite dynamic, features and updates are pushed out into releases almost every day for first 6 months (it is less frequent now, about once a week). A large percentage of features requested by the customers were implemented within the same day, and becomes available the next day. This is possible because the code is clean and simple (after constantly refactoring).

There were defects, but rarely major or critical thanks to the automated testing. A ClinicWise build must pass all automated tests. The customer never saw the same defect twice. This, in my opinion, is critically important. Whether they like it or not, most software users are used to software defects. They can tolerate software bugs to a certain extent, but not when the same error keeps occurring, which will destroy their confidence in the product. The best way to prevent recurring errors is regression testing. And the best way to do regression testing is to automate it.

Some other dentists saw ClinicWise at my relative's clinic, they liked it and signed up, so did my physiotherapist. They even compared ClinicWise favourably against major vendors.

I will share you the five stages of ClinicWise development here.

Build Stats

Let me start with showing the stats of ClinicWise's full build.

[1]https://clinicwise.net

Over 200,000 test executions over 600 days

This number is not that big, mostly because all the work was done in my spare time.

> **Build time** | **UI Test Cases** | **UI Test Stats**
>
> Builds: **1077**
> Total test case executions: **215081**
> Total execution time: **39 days 6 hours**
> Pass rate: **96.8%**
> Date range: 2013-03-31 to 2015-01-03 (643 days 9 hours)

374 comprehensive automated UI test cases

The number of automated UI tests increases gradually along with the development. By the way, there are 188 page classes used in the test scripts.

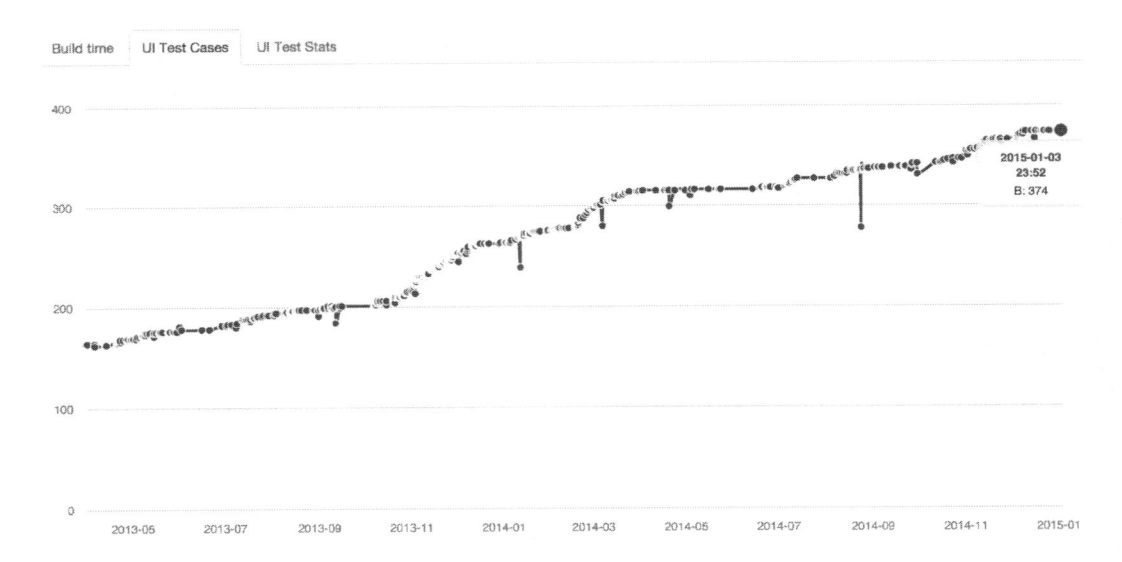

Build time

If an end-to-end test takes 20 seconds to run on average, a build would take over 2 hours to complete executing all 374 tests. This is too long!

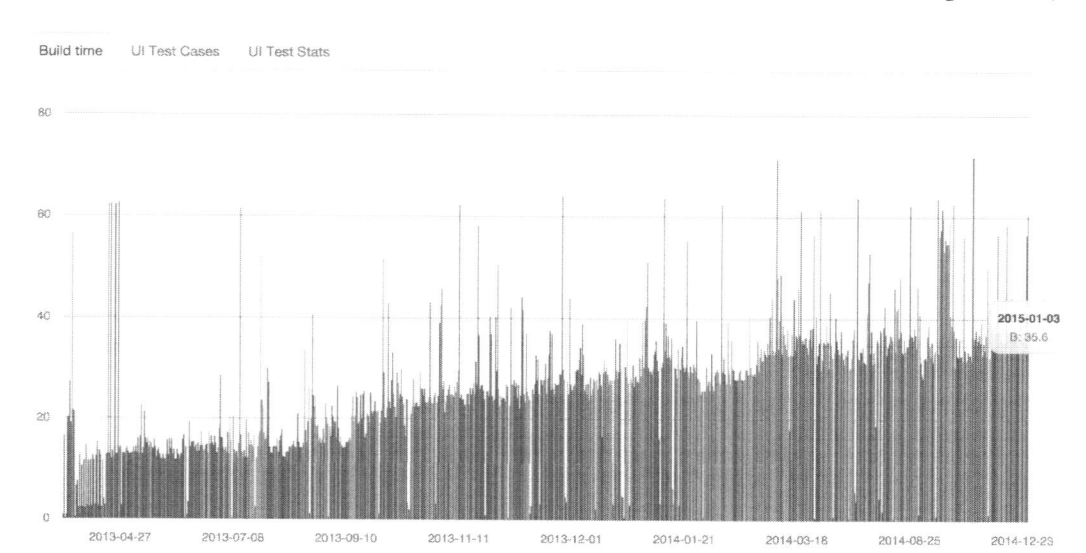

ClinicWise's CI process employs 6 build agents to speed up the full build (running all tests).

There are a lot of information we can get from the above chart. Many failed builds (in red) happened at the beginning when the code was under constant big changes. When it becomes more stabilised, even with more tests, we can see higher percentage of green builds. More importantly, there are always failed builds over the whole period (the same for other projects I involved), which means that the testing process has been detecting defects effectively.

Test Automation enables Agile

Over the years, the automated UI test suite enabled me the flexibility to keep improving the software. Here are some notable changes:

- Upgrade Rails 3 to 4.0, then 4.2 (underneath web framework)
- Upgrade to BootStrap 3 (UI framework)
- Ruby 1.9 to 2.0, then 2.1 (programming language)
- Major web design changes: twice
- Switch production web server from Apache to Nginx (deployment)
- Upgrade to Passenger 4 (deployment framework)
- Cross browser testing (Firefox and Chrome)
- 300+ database migrations (yes, database structure changes)

- Many new features and enhancements
- A dozen of major refactorings

Without the automated tests, I wouldn't be able to achieve the majority of them.

Stage 1: Write automated tests on the first day

I don't follow the strict ATDD practice (writing an automated test before coding). In fact, I usually write automated UI tests while developing a feature. After writing an automated test for the feature you are building, you can use them to speed up verification during the development (usually programmers don't get it right on the first go). Many programmers don't realize that automated testing saves time when implemented at the initial stage of software development.

I used the practices such as page objects and test refactorings covered in this book.

The tools:

- TextMate, programmer editor on Mac
- TestWise, testing IDE

Stage 2: Set up CI server within the first week

TestWise has a test suite feature to allow executing multiple test script files, I seldom use it. As a matter of fact, I rarely ran more than one test script file in the testing IDE. It is much easier to let the CI server (in my case, BuildWise) run all the tests for you. Besides efficiency, it feels good that there is another hand you out while you are working on other tasks.

There are many CI servers on the market (free and commercial), but I only found a few support executing UI tests well. It is no surprises to me, as very few projects do automated UI testing well.

Setting up BuildWise to run RSpec tests is easy. See Chapter 11 for instructions.

Stage 3: Release to production early

The first release of ClinicWise was made to the production after a total of 40 hours of coding and testing (mind you, I don't separate testing from coding. To me, they are equally important unless the application requires no maintenance). It was not a coding marathon, a few hours each night and more hours on weekends. There was no target deadline either (i.e. no pressure). I just wanted to release the application with minimum features but still useful for the customer.

Here are the main features in the first production release:

- User Authentication
- User Authorization
- User management: add new user with role
- Patient management: add/edit new patient
- Appointment management: book new appointment on dairy
- Register service items with pricing information
- Practitioners record treatment notes and then select service items for billing
- Receptionists issue invoice and accept payment

There are some common components, such as user authentication, that I could leverage with well established libraries and my pervious experience. For features specific to clinic management, I focused on the must-have ones. I started simple with each feature. For example, "registering a new client", I didn't implement the calendar date picker for inputing the birth date field, nor the calculation of the age. These can come later. It was only a text box entry in the first release.

Stage 4: Release often (daily)

Once the software was in production, I instantly got feedback and some defect reports (sent to me by the system automatically with full error stack trace). I dealt with the defects first.

I am not fixated on pushing out exactly one release a day. I release a good build (passed all tests) anytime I like as long as the timing is convenient for the customers. After all, if you do the same thing often, you will do it with confidence and little stress.

One year later, ClinicWise is still released to production regularly as shown below. One release under each folder was named by the deployment time.

```
Jan 30 21:20 20140130212011/
Feb  2 12:03 20140202120252/
Feb  5 04:52 20140205045050/
Feb  5 21:36 20140205213549/
Feb  6 20:59 20140206205844/
Feb  7 21:16 20140207211551/
Feb 10 00:00 20140209235958/
Feb 11 21:47 20140211214714/
Feb 18 07:24 20140213210551/
Feb 19 23:38 20140219233540/
Feb 20 21:50 20140220214914/
Feb 21 21:11 20140221211103/
Feb 23 22:43 20140223224240/
Feb 24 21:44 20140224214323/
Feb 25 22:13 20140225221245/
Feb 26 22:16 20140226221542/
Feb 27 23:56 20140227235502/
Mar  1 23:40 20140301234021/
```

Stage 5: Set up parallel test execution in CI

As the number of tests grew rapidly, so was the time taken to run all UI tests. The best solution, in my opinion, is to distribute automated tests to multiple build machines to execute them in parallel. The reason is simple, it is scalable.

I set up 6 build machines (in Virtual Machine images). When a full build started, tests were assigned to them to execute. This way, the total time was greatly reduced.

Duration: **35 minutes**

▽ Build artifacts
    build.log 54KB
    changeset.log 3KB

▷ Change log

▽ Acceptance Test Results (374 test cases , 2 hours 50 minutes) | Export Excel , CSV

AGENT	TEST FILE - TEST CASES (in 141 test scripts files)	TIME (S)	RESULTS	PRIORITY
BWA-iMac-07	calendar_rebook_spec.rb	99.6	Rerun	35
	- Calendar - Rebook Rebook a similar appointment from existing one	40.5	OK	
	- Calendar - Rebook Rebook a client group appointment	44.1	OK	
BWA-iMac-06	holidays_spec.rb	76.5	Rerun	35
	- Holidays Create a new holiday - one day, and edit	20.4	OK	
	- Holidays Create hoilday span over multiple days	17.9	OK	
	- Holidays Admin can show and add standard holidays; delete holiday remove calendar event	23.9	OK	
BWA-iMac-08	notices_spec.rb	149.1	Rerun	35

(Run against different browers on build agents)

The above screenshot shows that

- 374 tests would take 2 hours and 50 minutes on one build machine. Now it takes only 35 minutes (including the time for checking out and deployment) with 6 build machines
- Different build machines (named differently, e.g. BWA-Mini-02, BWA-iMac-11) participated in the build
- You may assign a BuildWise Agent to run against a specific type of browser: Firefox, Chrome or IE.

Questions and Answers

Q: What test frameworks do you use?

RWebSpec with Selenium WebDriver and Watir (against IE on Windows only) underneath. I started with supporting Chrome, Firefox and IE. As the time goes on, I found ClinicWise customers were quite happy to switch to Chrome or Firefox for faster browsing experience. So I dropped the testing in IE. As a result, some of the new test scripts only works with Selenium WebDriver.

Q: What application do you use for defect management ?

Nothing. Whenever a defect was found (regardless the source), I added an automated test case (or added more test steps in an existing test) to replicate the defect. Then worked to fix the code to pass the test, then trigger a build on BuildWise to run all tests.

Q: How do you do test reporting?

Nothing particularly. I regularly check BuildWise CI server for test reports.

Q: How do you do cross browser testing?

It is quite easy with BuildWise agents. In fact, I don't need to do much at all. On one build agent, I set the browser preference of one BuildWise Agent to 'Firefox', and the rest to 'Chrome' (As ClinicWise customers are advised to use Chrome and Firefox. To add testing IE, the same way). During a build, different tests are allocated to build agents. As the regression tests were run by BuildWise regularly, it does take long for the tests to run on Firefox and Chrome. I did need to add some custom scripts to do differently based on the browser type.

Q: What's the total cost to set up your build-and-test lab?

Hardware:

- A MacMini, served as the repository server (Git) and CI Server (BuildWise)
- An iMac, as the main development computer, with 3 Build VMs.
- Another MacMini, 3 Build VMs

Software:

- TestWise IDE Mac edition ($99) or TestWise Professional for Windows (from $249)
- BuildWise CI Server, free
- 6 Windows XP licenses
- Parallels Desktop virtualization software to run Windows VMs
- 6 BuildWise Agent licenses (in Windows VMs), $199 each

As a matter of fact, with effort, you can achieve the above setup (excluding hardware) at no cost.

- Use TestWise Community Edition, Apatana Studio (or other IDEs supporting Ruby) to run or edit Selenium-RSpec test scripts
- BuildWise Server for CI server
- Virtual Box virtualization software and test VMs[2]

---

[2] https://www.modern.ie/en-us/virtualization-tools#downloads

- Applying free (up to 5) Windows licenses from BizSpark[3], or reuse your old PC licenses. For large build farms, MSDN Operating Systems subscription subscription[4] offers best value and convenience.
- Use Linux build VMs
- Read BuildWise server code, develop your own build agent (command line version is not difficult to implement).

Q: How do you value the test automation and CI for ClinicWise? Does it really achieve what Simon Stewart said at STARWEST 2015 - "an order of magnitude more effective[5]."

For ClinicWise, what I can say is, without automated testing and CI, there would be no ClinicWise. In this sense, I agree with Mr. Stewart. Besides productivity (even our customers were surprised. They couldn't believe the feature that they requested was completed very next day. I really enjoyed the peace of mind and flexibility in developing ClinicWise.

If you really want to get a number (in terms of how effective does test automation and CI bring to the project), I can tell you the feedback from two software projects that I mentored. The two project managers happened to tell me the same finding: the whole team is about 3 times more productive after the test automation and CI was in place.

---

[3] http://www.microsoft.com/bizspark/
[4] https://www.visualstudio.com/en-us/products/msdn-os-vs
[5] http://starwest.techwell.com/sme-profiles/simon-stewart

Resources

Books

- **Watir Recipes**[6] by Zhimin Zhan

    The problem solving guide to Watir with over 100 ready to run recipe test scripts.
- **Selenium WebDriver Recipes in Ruby**[7] by Zhimin Zhan

    The problem solving guide to Selenium WebDriver with over 100 ready to run recipe test scripts.
- **Learn Ruby Programming by Examples**[8] by Zhimin Zhan and Courtney Zhan

    Master Ruby programming to empower you to write test scripts.

Web Sites

- **Selenium Ruby API** (http://selenium.googlecode.com/git/docs/api/rb/index.html[9])

    The API has searchable interface, The *SearchContext* and *Element* class are particularly important:
    - SearchContext[10]
    - Element[11]
- **HTML Elements supported by Watir**[12]
- **Selenium Home**[13]
- **RSpec**[14]
- **Cucumber**[15]
- **Watir WebDriver**[16]

---

[6] https://leanpub.com/watir-recipes
[7] https://leanpub.com/selenium-recipes-in-ruby
[8] https://leanpub.com/learn-ruby-programming-by-examples-en
[9] http://selenium.googlecode.com/git/docs/api/rb/index.html
[10] http://selenium.googlecode.com/git/docs/api/rb/Selenium/WebDriver/SearchContext.html
[11] http://selenium.googlecode.com/git/docs/api/rb/Selenium/WebDriver/Element.html
[12] https://github.com/watir/watir/wiki/HTML-Elements-Supported-by-Watir
[13] http://seleniumhq.org
[14] http://rspec.info
[15] http://cukes.info
[16] http://watirwebdriver.com

Tools

- **TestWise IDE**[17]

    AgileWay's next generation functional testing IDE supports Selenium, Watir with RSpec and Cucumber. TestWise Community Edition is free.

- **Apatana Studio**[18]

    Free Eclipse based Web development IDE, supporting Ruby and RSpec.

- **BuildWise**[19]

    AgileWay's free and open-source continuous build server, purposely designed for running automated UI tests with quick feedback.

- **RubyShell**[20]

    A pre-packaged Windows installer for Ruby and automated testing gems includes Selenium, RSpec and Cucumber. Free.

---

[17] [http://testwisely.com/testwise

[18] http://aptana.com

[19] http://testwisely.com/buildwise

[20] http://testwisely.com/testwise/downloads

References

[Crispin & Gregory 09] Lisa Crispin and Janet Gregory. 2009. *Agile Testing.* Addison-Wesley Progressional.

[Shore & Warden 08] James Shore and Shane Warden. *The Art of Agile Development.* 2008. O'Reilly Media Inc.

[Hunt & Thomas 00] Andrew Hunt and David Thomas. 2000. *The Programatic Programmer: From Journeyman to Master.* Addison-Wesley Progressional.

[Fowler et al. 99] Martin Fowler, Kent Beck, John Brant, William Opdyke, Don Roberts. "Refactoring: Improving the Design of Existing Code", Addison-Wesley Progressional.

[Fowler 00] Matrin Folwer, "Continuous Integration (original version)" (posted Sep 10, 2010) http://martinfowler.com/articles/originalContinuousIntegration.html

http://martinfowler.com/articles/continuousIntegration.html

[Crispin 07] Lisa Crispin, "To Track or Not to Track", *http://lisacrispin.com/downloads/TrackOrNot.pdf*

[Crispin 08] Lisa Crispin, "The Team's Pulse: CI/Build Process" (posted on Aug 23, 2010) http://lisacrispin.com/wordpress/2010/08/23/the-teams-pulse-cibuild-process/

[NEWS 11b] "Queensland Health payroll will cost up to $220 million to fix, acting director-general admits". Jul 14, 2011. *http://www.couriermail.com.au/news/queensland/queensland-health-payroll-will-cost-up-to-220-million-to-fix-acting-director-general-admits/story-e6freoof-1226094095536*

[NEWS 10a] "Pay system not properly tested: report", Jun 29, 2010. http://www.computerworld.com.au/article/351475/pay_system_properly_tested_report/#closeme

[Calzolari et al, 98] F. Calzolari, P. Tonella and G. Antoniol. 1998. "Dynamic Model for Maintenance and Testing Effort". Software Maintenance, 1998. Proceedings.

[Wells 09] Don Wells, "The Values of Extreme Programming" *http://www.extremeprogramming.org/values.html*

[NEWS 11c] "What would Larry Page do? Leadership lessons from Google's doyen". April 18, 2011.
http://management.fortune.cnn.com/2011/04/18/what-would-larry-page-do-leadership-lessons-from-google's-doyen/

[Cockburn 04] Alistair Cockburn. 2004. http://groups.yahoo.com/group/scrumdevelopment/message/2977?threaded=1&p=25

[Feathers 10] Michael Feathers. "UI Test Automation Tools are Snake Oil", Object Mentor Blog (posted on Jan 4 2010). *http://blog.objectmentor.com/articles/2010/01/04/ui-test-automation-tools-are-snake-oil*

[IDT07] Bernie Gauf and Elfriede Dustin. 2007. "The Case for Automated Software Testing". *http://journal.thedacs.com/issue/43/90*

[AAFTT 09] AAFTT Workshop 2009. *http://cds43.wordpress.com/2009/10/06/aaftt-workshop-2009-chicago/*

[AAFTTVW 07] Agile Alliance Functional Testing Tools Visioning Workshop. 2007. *http://www.infoq.com/news/2007/10/next-gen-functional-testing*

[Myers, Glenford 04]. The Art of Software Testing. Wiley. ISBN 978-0471469124.

[FSF] The Free Software Definition, http://www.gnu.org/philosophy/free-sw.html

Made in the USA
Middletown, DE
02 March 2016